101
Secrets for a Great Retirement

Practical, Inspirational, & Fun Ideas
for the Best Years of Your Life

Mary Helen and **Shuford Smith**

McGraw·Hill

New York   Chicago   San Francisco   Lisbon   London   Madrid   Mexico City
Milan   New Delhi   San Juan   Seoul   Singapore   Sydney   Toronto

*The **McGraw·Hill** Companies*

Library of Congress Cataloging-in-Publication Data

Smith, Mara.
      101 secrets for a great retirement / Mara and Ford Smith.
          p.   cm.
      Includes index.
      ISBN 0-7373-0420-0
        1. Retirement—Planning.   I. One hundred one secrets for a great retirement.
  II. Title: One hundred and one secrets for a great retirement.   III. Smith, Ford.
  IV. Title.

      HQ1062 .S62   2000
      646.7'9—dc21   00-032328

   10 11 12 13 14 15 16 17 18   DOC/DOC   0 9 8 7

ISBN 0-7373-0420-0

McGraw-Hill books are available at special quantity discounts to use as premiums and sales promotions, or for use in corporate training programs. For more information, please write to the Director of Special Sales, Professional Publishing, McGraw-Hill, Two Penn Plaza, New York, NY 10121-2298. Or contact your local bookstore.

This book is printed on acid-free paper.

To the retirees of Tryon, NC,
who knowingly, and unknowingly,
contributed to this book

Contents

Letter to Reader   *xi*

PART ONE
Make Successful Transitions   **1**

  1. Realize We Are in Charge of Our Lives and Happiness   3
  2. Accept That Retirement Brings Changes   4
  3. Embrace the Natural Process of Aging   6
  4. Face Crucial Life Issues   7
  5. Develop a Well-Thought-Out Philosophy   9
  6. Find a Balance   10
  7. Know the Difference Between High Quality of   11
      Life and High Standard of Living
  8. Simplify Life   13
  9. Evaluate All Options   14
 10. Visualize Life in Twenty Years   15
 11. Make Meaningful Commitments   16
 12. Retire to *Something*   17
 13. Expect Realized Dreams to Differ from Fantasies   19

PART TWO
Maintain Strong Financial and Legal Resources   **21**

 14. Understand Our Personal Relationship with Money   23
 15. Plan a Financial Future and How to Get There   24
 16. Investigate Government Programs for Retirees   26
 17. Allocate and Spend Money Wisely   27
 18. Think Through Long-Term Needs   28
 19. Recalculate Insurance   30
 20. Be a Savvy Consumer   31
 21. Save   33
 22. Balance Investment Returns with Risk Factors   35
 23. Know When Enough Is Enough   36

24. Learn to Give   38
25. Leave a Legacy   39
26. Organize Legal Affairs   41
27. Know Legal Options   43
28. Lower Risk of Crime   44

PART THREE
Develop Optimum Health   **47**

29. Get in Touch with the Body   49
30. Realize Intelligence Evolves with Age   50
31. Apply New, Positive Habits   52
32. Practice Preventive Medicine   53
33. Pay Attention to Diet   55
34. Stay Active   57
35. Exercise   58
36. Avoid Hazardous Products and Situations   60
37. Learn What to Do in Emergencies   61
38. Know Options for Medical Treatment   62
39. Discern Between Viable Choices and Hoaxes   64
40. Prepare Medical Directives   65

PART FOUR
Build Emotional Strength   **69**

41. Regulate Emotional States to Enhance Health   71
and Life Span
42. Learn to Live Happily   72
43. Develop a Positive Attitude and Open Mind   73
44. Show Appreciation and Gratitude   75
45. Challenge Irrational Beliefs   76
46. Recognize Brainwashing   77
47. Practice Relaxation Techniques   79
48. Face Fears   80
49. Accept Death   81
50. Understand the Process of Grief   82

CONTENTS

PART FIVE
Seek Vital Relationships   85

51. Express Love and Kindness   87
52. Seek Out Other Happy People   88
53. Become a Better Listener   89
54. Improve Existing Friendships   91
55. Make New Friends   92
56. Enjoy Sex   93
57. Enrich the Marriage   94
58. Support Our Partners in Achieving Personal Dreams and Pleasures   96
59. Adjust the Role of Parenting   97
60. Understand the Role of Grandparenting   99
61. Help Parents and Other Older People   100
62. Give Up the Myth of the Happy Family   102
63. Be the First to Forgive   103
64. Bond Again   104
65. Consider a Pet   106
66. Connect with the Natural World   107

PART SIX
Choose Enriching Activities   109

67. Master What Brings Pleasure   111
68. Stretch the Pleasure Quotient   112
69. Explore Hobbies and Recreational Activities   114
70. Do Something Wild   115
71. Take Small Steps Toward New Endeavors   116
72. Keep Learning   118
73. Contemplate, Read Books, Join Discussions— Expand Mentally   119
74. Learn How to Use a Computer   120
75. Record Life Experiences   122
76. Attend Social Gatherings and Cultural Activities   123
77. Travel with Focus and Spirit   124

CONTENTS

78. Consider Work After Retiring — 125
79. Volunteer — 127
80. Follow a Passion — 129
81. Get Involved in Meaningful Activity — 130
82. Take Action — 131
83. Develop More Persistence — 132
84. Store Up Good Memories — 133

PART SEVEN
Create Quality Living Space — **135**
85. Know What Makes a Good Home — 137
86. Surround Ourselves with Beauty — 138
87. Reduce Clutter — 139
88. Consider All Housing Options — 141
89. Relocate Realistically — 142

PART EIGHT
Boost Potential — **145**
90. Have Great Expectations — 147
91. Convert Negatives into Positives — 148
92. Confront Old-Age Stereotypes — 149
93. Heighten Curiosity — 151
94. Live in the Moment — 152
95. Make Time an Ally — 153
96. Stay Engaged with Life — 155
97. Practice Resiliency — 156
98. Know We Can Change at Any Age — 157
99. Realize Opportunities to Be by Oneself — 158
100. Become Wise — 160
191. Make Life the Best — 161

Afterword — *163*

Dear Reader,

When we were researching our first book on retirement, *The Retirement Sourcebook*, we were puzzled that so much information on retirement deals with financial, legal, medical, and demographic issues. Article after article talks about how to retire rich. More articles, and even books, list "approved" places to retire. The majority of information is concerned with money or where to live. Many retirement books are catalogued under aging. In *The Retirement Sourcebook*, we took a holistic approach to the many aspects of retirement (challenges, health and well-being matters, social and emotional changes, work and play opportunities, financial and legal issues, safety and security concerns). In this book, we look at what distinguishes a great retirement from an average or sorry one.

Financial, legal, medical, and demographic information are important. We were fortunate to discover after our early retirement, at ages thirty-nine and forty-three, that we needed less money than we had saved. In our preparation, we had not ignored legal and medical issues. In fact, we found that meeting them head-on made us feel in control of our health and carefree about the dispensation of our possessions. We disregarded information on where to live. Instead, we elected to travel across North America for ten years, creating our own short list of potential retirement places.

In our retirement, we've enjoyed very rich lives. Firsthand through our experiences and secondhand through our acquaintances, we became aware that there were lots of secrets to a great retirement. Retirees we gravitated toward were active, involved, satisfied, and happy. They were positive; they were vibrant. They were a delight to get to know.

Yet, as we traveled, shopped for our groceries, laundered our clothes, and performed other routine chores, we encountered others who were experiencing mediocre retirements. Many retirees were so bored that they were filling time with low-paying jobs. These individuals appeared to be growing in number. We felt that this was a disturbing trend given the U.S. Census statistic that the ranks of American retirees were swelling by 6,500 a day!

What were the differences between happy and not-so-happy retirees? As we met with other retirees and visited recommended retirement locales, we determined that neither net worth nor location was critical to happiness. More important were factors such as attitude, resolve, and emotional maturity. In other words, people could enjoy a great retirement without a net worth of a million dollars or a home in a retirement community.

In this book, we list those secrets and write a few words to share what we've learned. We've garnered additional facts from academic research, organizational surveys, and personal interviews. To be included in our book, each secret had to "ring true." It had to be observable and verifiable by people enjoying a great retirement.

Although the secrets are written as individual essays, they are grouped together in broad categories: making successful transitions, maintaining strong financial and legal resources, developing optimum health, building emotional strength, seeking vital relationships, choosing enriching activities, creating quality living space, and boosting potential. Each section contains information that will help you achieve a great retirement. No part is more important than another but you may find that one group of essays, or even a particular essay, contains the key you need to open up your retirement years. If many of these secrets appear to be common sense, that's great. It means we are building on familiar concepts.

You may prefer to read this book straight through, marking applicable ideas. You may find it helpful to read one section at a time and reflect on it. Or, perhaps you'll want to scan, looking for that missing something holding you back from doing what you want in your retirement. In our essays, you may find the secret that unlocks a great retirement. We hope our tips will give you new perspectives and motivation. We all benefit from inspirational moments, such as someone telling us we can do something right at a time when we're in doubt. These secrets may serve as a coach or counselor. You can study the secrets with a friend or mate. You can refer to them again and again.

Written for retirees looking for encouragement, future retirees planning ahead, as well as friends and family members looking for the perfect gift for a retiree, this book gives the essence of each secret to a great retirement. For most people, that will be enough. If more information is required, such as contacts, references, statistics, and studies, check out our resource book, *The Retirement Sourcebook*.

In this letter and in the afterword, *we* refers to us as the authors. In our essays, *we* refers to all of us as retirees or future retirees. We're all experiencing this amazing time together. Get ready to enjoy retirement to its fullest.

Our best,

Mary Helen and Shuford Smith

PART ONE

Make Successful Transitions

"*Retirement may be one of the greatest changes in our lives and offer us one of the greatest challenges. Yet, for most of us, we've only considered how much money we've saved and what trip we'd like to take.*"

RETIREE, AGED SIXTY-THREE

1 Realize We Are in Charge of Our Lives and Happiness

If we truly desire a great retirement, we come to one inescapable conclusion: it's our choice. We share one commonality: the same amount of time in each day of our lives. During those moments, we make thousands of decisions. These decisions determine the course of our future. While the rest of the world will have an impact, it's the choices we make that decide our happiness. Niceties such as housing, recreational activities, pensions, and medical facilities are insignificant compared with our resolve to live a great life.

By the time we've reached the point of retirement, we accept that no one else is controlling our destiny. It was easy when we were young to ascribe that power to parents, teachers, coaches, even our peers. During our working years, spouses, children, bosses, neighbors, and friends would make demands on our time.

We have encountered people who avoid any responsibility for their life situations by blaming others. We don't have to look far to find people carping on the horrible government, irresponsible media, or another "awful" group. In retirement, these blames may be aimed toward Social Security, doctors, uncaring children, and the like. For a happier and more satisfying life, however, choose to stop blaming (and avoid people who do) right now.

Hopefully, we've already learned that our lives' direction is always the result of our own determinations. If we haven't, continuing a fast-paced, hectic schedule may not provide an opportunity for us to concentrate on our future direction. If so, we may want to do what Thoreau did—go to the woods—or to a beach, desert, or mountaintop. When we remove ourselves from distractions, the nonverbal side of our intelligence—often called intuition—has a chance to express itself. We can discover answers to daily problems and address the bigger issues of what to do with the rest of our lives.

When we listen to both our rational brains and our intuitive hearts, we make better decisions. We realize that we have thousands of options, not just a handful of choices. We begin to live deliberately. It's up to each of us to take charge—for the rest of our lives.

2 Accept That Retirement Brings Changes

Retirement brings many changes; it's an ongoing process. What's more, our retirement phase can last for more than thirty years. It's time to get ready for the changes and put some effort into our plans for this challenging future.

It helps to understand that at the initial point of retirement, most of us have reasonable health, lots of energy, and ample money. We may dream of traveling, indulging hours in a favorite sport or hobby, or having loads of time to just putter around. We need to add to our planning process the understanding that at some point this very independent life may have to be altered: we or someone close to us may require additional support.

When we first switch into retirement mode, it makes sense to allow ourselves time for the transition. During this period, we test dreams, explore options, and experiment. When we find that one of our choices is not working (and we will), we adjust. If we're careful, we avoid getting trapped in an arrangement that can't be easily changed. The balancing act includes saying "no" as well as becoming actively involved. In addition, we prepare ourselves mentally for the needs of aging parents, demands of adult children, or the death of someone close.

We make it a priority to monitor our daily lives for possible areas of improvement. We ask, "What would make me feel better?" The answers come in the form of a change we can make. The status quo does not improve our lot. Change is the antithesis of blaming and complaining—it's taking charge of our lives. "I'll do it later" is a phrase we need to abandon. The time is now. If we dream of being a writer, we start writing today. If we want to improve our health, we add a bit of exercise or cut out an unhealthy snack today. It's up to each of us to take action.

One retiree wanted to simplify her life so she would have time to paint watercolors and ride horses. While she said this was her goal, she allowed herself to be influenced by others to apply for a position putting her organizational skills to good use for the community. Once hired and trained, she found herself unhappy because the job did not make her feel better about herself. She had postponed what she really wanted to do. For a year, she worked hard and improved the organization's membership lists, mailings, and fund-raising. During that time, she decided that if she could restructure an organization so well, surely she could do the same thing for herself. She resigned, rewarding herself with time for her first horse and her watercolors.

The better we become at implementing our changes, the more we enjoy our retirement years. To make successful changes, we must identify our goals, make a firm commitment to those goals, then take steps toward them. Some steps may be uncomfortable and hard. It's important to realize that these steps are leading in a positive direction for us. When we take charge of our lives by implementing necessary changes, we discover satisfaction, contentment, and exhilaration.

3 Embrace the Natural Process of Aging

Each of us is growing older every second, minute, and hour of the day. It's a natural process. We choose whether to embrace or deny our own aging. Those of us who understand the process and adapt to its challenges are likely to be happy with our decisions. Those of us who refuse to face our fears about growing old tend to be unhappy with the resulting ambivalence in our lives.

It sounds like a simple recipe for happiness—accept aging, this natural process we cannot change—but it's not so easy. In our minds, we still feel young. We have strong memories of how we once looked and how we wish to look, of what we were able to accomplish and what we hope still to accomplish. These feelings can trick us into not accepting reality.

As we encounter conditions that diminish our physical vitality, we need to be aware of how to improve our situations as well as ameliorate our feelings. Books, Web sites, senior centers, government offices, and medical organizations provide information about aging. Some lending libraries offer a collection of helpful products. Examine amplified and large-button telephones, extra-loud alarm clocks, talking watches, giant timers, and magnifiers. It's helpful to study these aids, learning what they can and can't do to enhance our lives. If we find ourselves depressed about a particular situation, we may need more than what publications or products can offer. We may want to talk to medical specialists, see counselors, or become involved with support groups.

Many of us first become aware of our aging by changes in our eyesight. Most people find they need reading glasses around age fifty. As our age increases, so does the corrective power of the lens. We may resort to magnifying glasses and other optical aids. In the near future, we may be able to opt for corrective laser surgery.

Next, we start to wonder about that face in the mirror. It's sagging around the mouth, creating an unhappy look. We can perform facial exercises. Such toning and tightening may last longer than any face lift. Certainly, exercises are less invasive and expensive.

If we're hearing less and less, we need to determine the cause of the loss. It could be as simple as a buildup of earwax. It could be more permanent. We need to know if a hearing aid will help. Specially equipped phones might be beneficial, too. To connect with people, we may need to hone our writing skills, using paper, a small blackboard, or a computer for printed and electronic communications.

If we begin to lose our senses of smell and taste, we must learn how to compensate with different aromas and spices that bring us pleasure.

If our short-term memories fail us on occasion, we must develop the habit of writing down important things and making lists as necessary.

We may experience one or more of these failings. We may experience other physical problems. Informed, we can make decisions that will enable us to continue to enjoy our retirement.

The challenge of growing older is to do it gracefully. It helps to know what's ahead. It helps to know the many options for diminished capacities. It helps to not worry or complain about what cannot be changed. It helps to work persistently at what can be changed. Throughout our retirement, it helps to maintain an attitude of staying fully engaged with life.

4 Face Crucial Life Issues

If we feel our lives have simply been happening to us rather than our directing them, that's a sign we need to face up to critical life issues. At many times in our lives, each of us encounters happiness, love, forgiveness, responsibility, marriage, children, society, poverty, wealth, greed, power, fear, aggression, war, aging, death, and spirituality. Philosophers have spent their lives struggling with these ideas. How about us?

Retirement offers us one last opportunity to assess how we've been dealing with these life topics. Have we merely coped with these issues or have we faced them head-on, mastering our thoughts and feelings, knowing what actions we would take?

It's easy to float along, letting events happen, making decisions based only on what's at hand. This may be easy, but it's probably not the most fulfilling way to approach our lives. And, if we never get around to dealing with how we feel about life and its many varied aspects, we may develop neurotic behaviors that mask our emotions from others—and ourselves.

How does one go about facing life issues like the ones listed above? The answer depends on our personal histories. If one has experienced great trauma and has buried feelings about a problem, this individual may need therapy. Most people, however, benefit from reading, listening to audiocassettes, watching video productions, and talking to family members and friends.

Explore one or more of these life issues at a time. Books and other productive materials help us understand these concepts. Think about how each topic has affected our personal experiences. What feelings come to the surface? Write down these thoughts and feelings in a journal. Putting words on paper may help us work through problems. Often, matters are interrelated, such as love and marriage. Our experiences might involve more than one subject at a time. Study the interconnections. Come to new understandings.

One retiree, whose wife died suddenly, shared that he wrestled with issues of death, love, marriage, responsibility, and happiness for over a year. It wasn't until a friend asked for help with a personal problem that the retiree began to take action. With this new involvement, his own understandings and feelings fell into place.

In our retirement, we want to visualize ourselves effectively handling crucial issues. Deliberately, we can work toward that model, becoming stronger players in the game of life.

5 Develop a Well-Thought-Out Philosophy

As children, we play make-believe. Becoming adults, we make beliefs. It's important to understand, choose, then live our values. They are the structure that supports us through all our experiences, whether negative, positive, or in-between. One retiree expresses the concept this way: "I've come to realize that people who have mastered life seem to be guided by an internal compass. They've developed a philosophy that always brings them back on course."

While some behaviors are continuous throughout our lives, other functions are more common in our later years. Always, we need to love and be loved, to forgive and be forgiven. In our retirement, we want to let go of old roles, to adjust to losses, to value wisdom above physical skills and charms. We desire to come to terms with our lives and prepare for our deaths.

Letting go of old roles is essential to finding different ways of relating to others. Let's face it: our children and grandchildren may want to hear of our career achievements once or twice, but not over and over again. Our parenting and grandparenting roles may change with retirement, too. Hopefully, we continue to take a less active parenting role and a more active grandparenting role.

Adjusting to losses includes adapting to changes in our senses, such as hearing and sight. It's accepting other changes in our bodies, too. We may no longer be able to run marathons. We must content ourselves with what we can do: maintain skills, improve others, and learn new ones. Other worrisome losses include friends and relatives, who may move away or die. We must allow ourselves to feel each loss, then strive to regain a new balance.

As we age, becoming less able and more wrinkled, we switch our focus from our physical qualities to our mental abilities. We value our wealth of past experiences, which will continue to help us make wise decisions.

Coming to terms with our lives and preparing for our deaths, we accept and value the human life process and our personal pasts. Thus, we are able to look ahead, accomplishing unfinished tasks, planning to die with dignity, arranging our memorial services, and leaving legacies.

Our own well-thought-out philosophy is the best course to lead us through these stages of life. Other people may provide good role models. Religion may be of comfort. But it's up to each of us to chart our path through retirement.

6 Find a Balance

Often, upon retiring, we have to find a new balance or center in our lives. We no longer carry important job titles and devote multitudinous hours to a career. We must find new ways to think about ourselves and different activities to look forward to each day.

Retirement can be a time of self-discovery. It's possible to become more self-reflective, getting to better know ourselves and accepting our "bad" parts as well as our "good" parts. One way to do this is to study personality typing systems such as the Enneagram or the Myers-Briggs. Such instruction helps us identify and understand behavior patterns in ourselves and others.

In this process of accepting ourselves, we become less judgmental of others, too. We learn to relax and lower our stress levels. We live more completely in the present moment, listening to others, balancing our private and social needs, learning when to say "yes" and when to say "no."

It all begins with self, though. It's important to affirm ourselves, nourishing our physical and mental needs, building a strong self-image, creating healthy lifestyle habits, and pursuing what we perceive to be a "good" life. Realizing the power within ourselves, we take charge and set goals. We see opportunities, relish leisure pursuits, enjoy changing relationships, devote time to others, and speak our minds.

Although we are free from our careers, there are roles that we'll continue to perform, such as being parents. We may want to consciously switch gears, however, adopting a more "hands-off" approach.

When we acknowledge our years, we must feel vital and proud to be as long-lived as we are. In addition, we give ourselves permission to look for new ways to feel productive about the rest of our lives.

In our retirement years, we can take off in exciting directions. It's a great time to look at all our dreams since childhood. It may be time to focus on one of these dreams. Our imaginations are our outer limits.

7 Know the Difference Between High Quality of Life and High Standard of Living

Confusing our standard of living with our quality of life is easy to do, regardless of age. We tend to expect our quality of life to go up whenever we buy another product or service. What's really going up, however, is our standard of living. Quality of life has nothing to do with having electricity, a refrigerator, a washer, a dryer, or a computer. Advertising may promise a better quality of life, but it doesn't deliver. Though a task may become more convenient, our lives remain the same.

Quality of life has more to do with the surroundings in which we choose to live. It's having a beautiful view outside our windows. It's displaying pretty flowers. It's serving fresh vegetables. It's eating homemade bread. It's drinking pure water. It's walking out the front door for a refreshing stroll. It's feeling secure enough to leave doors unlocked. It's delighting in the antics of animals. It's sharing smiles and kind words with neighbors. It's helping with a project that improves the community. It's appreciating and giving gratitude for these basic things that give us pleasure.

When we travel, we can see the differences between standard of living and quality of life. We discover that places with a low standard of living can score quite high on quality of life. For example, a rural home may have few modern appliances but enjoy an abundance of fresh fruits and vegetables.

Knowing the difference between standard of living and quality of life is especially helpful to retirees, who spend less time at their jobs and more time in and around their houses. By getting back to basics, we make our homes into places we really enjoy. By paying more attention to food and exercise, we enhance our day-to-day lives. For every endeavor, we ask, "Will this improve the quality of my life?"

If we relocate our homes, knowing what brings us pleasure and what raises our quality of life will help make decisions easier. This knowledge helps us find more suitable locations and structures. It assists in deciding which possessions to keep and which to let go.

More important, in seeking to raise our quality of life instead of our standard of living, we become more appreciative of life in general. In the process, we become happier retirees.

8 Simplify Life

Think back to a few of the beautiful, simple moments in our lives. They might include a gorgeous sunset panorama, reflective minutes by a creek or waterfall, a solitary walk in the desert, a thrilling mountaintop vista, or a relaxed vacation at a beach. As we deal with the frenzy of modern life, simplicity can equate with sanity.

People actually need very little: water, food, and shelter. Everything else we add to our lives can be called niceties, not necessities. At some point, these niceties begin to subtract from our quality of life because they demand too much. Each nicety added to our lives, be it a new gadget or a role, will extract a share of our attention. As these demands accumulate, at some point we'll find ourselves feeling fragmented, overwhelmed, and mired in a swamp of obligations.

Retirement is an excellent time to reconstruct a life that includes only the most important and essential aspects. By simplifying, we'll rediscover the thrill of each moment. Bigger is not always better and going faster is not always the best way to get somewhere. As many retirees will testify, the simple things are often the most satisfying. Thoreau writes, "Our life is frittered away by detail. Simplicity, simplicity, simplicity!"

The first step in simplification is to rid ourselves of unnecessary complexity. We need to focus and ask ourselves questions. Let's direct all our attention to each day and then to each small item within each day. Ask, "Is this activity bringing me joy?" and "Is it reducing the complexity of my life?" If the answers are no, then discard that component. Have high standards. Each and every endeavor must justify its intrusion into our lives. Don't keep it around because you've always done it that way. Scrutinize everyday chores for shortcuts or alternatives that will make life easier. If we find ourselves unable to find a simpler path, we might ask a friend or our partners for help.

As we trim out unrewarding aspects, we begin the second step of simplification: the enhancement of the remaining core activities. Make each meal special in some way. Take a more scenic route on the next short trip. Shop for designer clothing and other necessary items at thrift stores. Make doing nothing into quality time. By enriching these routine moments, we'll be constructing a more fulfilling life.

The number of toys cannot determine our happiness. Our busyness quotient may leave us feeling frazzled rather than fulfilled. Simplify, simplify, simplify—and reap the rewards of contentment.

9 Evaluate All Options

Retirement is not a one-time event. It's a lifestyle resulting from our choice to stop working and to enjoy the rewards of our labors. In order to make all the resulting transitions successful, we must acknowledge our dreams with full awareness of what's ahead. Throughout these "golden years," we will make decision after decision about our activities, our relationships, our health, our homes, and our financial and legal affairs. Each time, we must evaluate all our options.

Our goal needs to be to make each selection the best available at the time. To do that, we must stay engaged with life, maintaining an awareness of opportunities. We must develop good resources and ways of obtaining up-to-date information. We must learn to think broadly, desiring to improve the quality of our lives with satisfying experiences.

With each decision we make, we must ask ourselves, What are the consequences of this decision? What are the best-case and worst-case scenarios? We must also consider the prices connected to each potential solution. Realizing that, sometimes, the best option may cost little or no money, we become more independent of advertising and peer pressures. Thus, we continue to move toward our dreams.

Sometimes, being busy prevents us from thinking through a situation. Other times, we may be fearful of losing money or of what our friends might think. When we're feeling fearful or fragmented, it's easy to revert to past behaviors and habits. Instead, we need to get in touch with our personal needs, goals, and dreams, and think through all the possibilities.

Realize, too, that procrastination is a decision. Not doing anything has its own consequences—usually not as favorable as those from well-thought-out choices.

In our retirement years, we must continue to work toward personal dreams. We must search widely through all the possible choices before selecting the best course. We must be honest with ourselves about what personal qualities and abilities we have to obtain what we want. And, we must be realistic about the time and effort needed to achieve, then maintain, those dreams. It may be impossible to act upon all our dreams, but moving toward even one of them may be the best option for our lives.

10 Visualize Life in Twenty Years

When we reach the age of sixty-five, the odds are good—especially for women—that we will make it to eighty-five. When we consider our health and our bodies, therefore, think of them in the context of the long term. We can visualize ourselves active and mentally alert well into the future. What we eat and how we exercise will play vital roles in the quality of our lives. A great example is a retiree who has planned in detail his one-hundred-twentieth birthday. It includes a hike along a special section of the Appalachian Trail. Though his dream may be only that, he feels that his body responds to his expectations.

If we consider a move, the awareness that we can live for twenty or more years may alter our criteria. Weather might be a factor in where we desire to live, but nice weather will not compensate for twenty years of poor social support. We establish in our mind (or minds, if we are part of a couple) the kinds of relationships and opportunities we want to experience in our choice of locales. These desires will influence our decisions of whether and where to move far more than the weather patterns.

Thinking in a twenty-year span impacts how we view our financial plan, also. We invest for the future. Stocks can be a part of our portfolio; our assets do not all have to be income-producing instruments. Reduce expenses that deplete savings over time. Taking in 10 percent more than we spend is a good rule of thumb.

Viewing retirement as a lengthy phase of our lives will help us through times of grief and loneliness. We know there will be bright moments in the future. This perspective frees us to work at establishing our own domains. Over the years, we create a rich milieu that includes walks, hikes, dances, conversations, letters, books, discussion groups, and worthwhile projects. We take time to interact with nature. We put love and affection at the top of our lists. We attempt new ventures. We reflect. We show appreciation. We continue to make our dreams real.

11 Make Meaningful Commitments

When we retire, we encounter many people who think we have lots of time to help others. These people might be family members or neighbors. They could be members of organizations looking for volunteer assistance. Unless we've planned ahead and know how we want to spend our time, we may find ourselves overwhelmed by such requests. On the surface, each appeal may appear reasonable. In action, however, each summons takes more time than we think.

Suddenly, we have insufficient time to take care of our needs and pursue our dreams. As a result, we may find ourselves shirking an agreed-to responsibility. Others may question our word. If this happens, it's time to renegotiate the understanding.

We learn from our experiences and the practices of others. Here is what a few other retirees have to say on the subject of commitment:

"Words are important. I say, 'I will do it,' not 'I'll try to do it.' "

"I try to keep my promises no matter what. It's a matter of self-discipline."

"I don't make commitments I don't plan to keep."

"Sometimes, I will make conditional agreements. For example, I'll tell someone, 'I'll be there unless such and such happens.' "

"Always, I write down my appointments."

"At the time, not appearing or not doing something may seem to be a little matter. To others, honesty and dishonesty, even in little things, are not small matters."

We need to honor our commitments to ourselves, too. If we're committing to a dream, we must choose it every time we make a choice on how we spend our time. Sometimes, the choices feel continuous—hourly, if not daily. And if the dream is important to us, we must not allow others to talk us out of it.

Take care when making commitments. Ensure they are worthy of our time. Then, make sure that we mean what we say and that we do what we say.

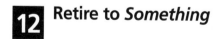 **Retire to *Something***

When people work at a job or perform a role, they have a focus. They have responsibilities. They have structure. To serve as a parent, storekeeper, salesperson, or mechanic demands certain actions on our part. During retirement, the scenario changes drastically. There is no schedule, no lists of tasks and obligations except those we create. For many, this void is the worst part of retirement. After several months of drifting, a sizable number leap back into the world of work to regain a sense of balance and purpose. The comment most often heard is, "I just wasn't ready."

There is much to learn from these aborted attempts at retirement. As individuals, we do find much of our self-esteem entwined with our tasks. When those tasks disappear, we become despondent. Much of our social life may be connected to the roles we've played. The role vanishes and we lose our contacts with others.

We need to find new dreams in retirement. We step away from old patterns and establish alternatives. We choose meaningful paths from a vast array of possibilities. What we cannot afford is to intend to start something but never take any action.

First, imagine, then visualize what we might do. Perhaps we want to be active grandparents, play golf or tennis, travel, volunteer, seek more solitary moments, paint, or write. The dreams vary widely. What doesn't vary is that these activities must satisfy us. They must meet our need to feel alive and to be of value. While it's easy enough to become busy—even busier than in preretirement years—the real challenge is to become immersed in fulfilling activity.

The secret of a successful transition is to follow dreams worthy of ourselves. How will we grandparent? Do we have a focus for travel? Are there significant projects for our volunteer efforts? Are we comfortable finding internal insights? Can we experiment with a creative interest, such as painting or woodworking? We're not trying to change the world; we are in the process of changing ourselves.

One retiree became a dedicated bicyclist rather than an occasional rider. He soon discovered that many city and country roads were unsafe due to the lack of a paved shoulder. He presented his case to the county commissioners and soon found scores of other bicyclists rallying behind him. A new organization was formed. Its members are meeting with success on city, county, and state levels.

When we establish this "something" to retire to, our lives take on new energy. And, we discover that retirement need not be a meaningless void.

13 Expect Realized Dreams to Differ from Fantasies

With new ventures such as travel, education, relocation, or writing the great American novel, we must realize that our experiences may not measure up to our dreams. We might endure a frustrating trip, encounter a poor teacher, find our new location full of unfriendly people, or run headlong into writer's block.

When we plan on a life that revolves around our favorite sport, we must anticipate how we'll adjust to injury (either our own or a partner's), boredom, or tension from overcompetitiveness.

When we hope to give back through volunteering, we must understand that many volunteer operations may be disorganized or staffed with less-than-dependable volunteers. And, society may view our efforts as somewhat unimportant since the work is unpaid.

When we envision ourselves happily involved in a new career, recognize that we may be seen as older workers to be patronized and underpaid. If we decide to be the next great entrepreneur and open a small business, we must realize that many are unprofitable, and that there is often no backup for us if we become ill or disabled.

When we elect to stay with our careers because of happiness or money, we must foresee the inevitable time when we can no longer continue (sudden incapacitation does occur). There will be many other rewarding opportunities, if we open ourselves to them.

In short, when we plan big and envision ourselves in perfect scenarios, we also must take off any blinders so we can glance at possible pitfalls. Have balanced expectations and be prepared to adjust and adapt.

PART TWO

Maintain Strong Financial and Legal Resources

"*Without a steady work income, retirement may lead to moments of money anxiety. When that happens to me, I remind myself of Thoreau's comment, 'Money is not required to buy one necessity of the soul.'* "

RETIREE, AGED SEVENTY-FOUR

14 Understand Our Personal Relationship with Money

Most of us retirees have grown up in societies consumed by money. The pursuit of wealth has become a fanatical religion to be followed without question. How many of us challenge the mantra "More is better"? Even the word *success* has become synonymous with money. All of us have been influenced by this barrage of money messages; we need to assess to what degree.

During retirement, much of our contentment will come from how well we understand our relationship with money. Have we traded part of our dreams for money? Will we continue to do so? Do we equate more money with more security, power, prestige, and social status? Do we live in fear of running out? Do we accumulate mainly to watch the numbers go higher? Do we spend without thinking? We need to look deep into our psyches to determine our true beliefs.

Somehow we must divorce ourselves from the general fear upon which economists thrive. Whether or not the inflation rate changes will probably have little impact on our daily lives. True security will not be found within any economic model. If we turn off all sources of financial news for a while, we find that our personal world really hasn't changed much at all.

Money has become so pervasive a concern that if we don't have a solid understanding of where we stand financially and where we're heading, we may experience great anxiety. First, realize a basic truth: wealthy people are no happier (or unhappier) than those with less money. Second, know that our only true personal asset is our time on Earth. We're trading that precious time for money—whether accumulating it or spending it. With those two tenets in mind, we can become more pragmatic in our future relationship with money.

We must treat retirement as the challenge of finding the best possible uses of the time we have left. Money will play only a minor role. We focus on experiencing all the special moments and pleasures that don't require an outlay of cash. We choose not to clutter up our lives with more stuff. We tell our children that our goal is to avoid becoming a financial burden on them, so they must not expect a large inheritance. We approach this stage of life using a scorecard based on satisfaction and joy rather than money.

15 Plan a Financial Future and How to Get There

Our financial picture shifts during our retirement years due not only to a change in income but also to the realities of a new lifestyle. Successful retirees have a solid understanding of the current situation as well as what the future might be. They set personal financial goals. All of us can do the same.

Naturally, our first consideration is to assure we have enough income to cover day-to-day expenses. We must realize that many expenses will change upon retirement. Many will be lower; others will be raised or added due to activities we choose to pursue. In one typical scenario, clothing, commuting, vehicle, housing, food, and tax costs are lower, while entertainment, travel, educational, and medical expenses are higher. When we add a new activity, we must recognize its effect on our budget (perhaps, the purchase of a new camera or walking shoes). We can also reduce our expenses when our living patterns change (fewer vehicles, smaller house, simpler clothes). When necessary, we may be able to produce additional income with options such as taking a part-time job, running a home business, or renting part of our houses.

Once we have today's budget covered, we must consider the effects of inflation. If food costs start rising at 10 percent each year, this would definitely affect our checkbooks. If the price of new houses takes off at that same 10 percent, it would impact us only if we were buying or selling. Instead of looking at an overall rate, we benefit by knowing where inflation is actually changing our day-to-day costs. Then, we adjust our plans.

Also, we need to consider the possible long-term medical and care needs of both ourselves and our partners. We need enough reserve to help cover these probable future expenses. Alas, there's no simple formula since there's no crystal ball. We garner information from various government programs and pension plans to add to our own resources. Then, we calculate a few different scenarios to see what we might need.

We must guard against the depletion of our resources that could occur due to volatility in the economic marketplace, fraud, or mismanagement. Remember investor basics: don't put money into something that's hard to understand, research before buying, choose quality and safety, diversify, stay calm, and understand that a professional manager may be less effective than common sense.

With all these considerations in mind, we develop a realistic financial plan. We ensure our plan's success by keeping our expenses closely attuned to our desires while cutting out the excess. We take advantage of any government assistance. We save and invest wisely. And, to keep us from becoming too obsessed with money, we recall the comments of one master money adviser, John Templeton: "Spiritual wealth is more important than monetary wealth."

16 Investigate Government Programs for Retirees

Many countries in the world today offer assistance to those beyond retirement age. All retirees benefit from understanding these programs to ensure they have taken the necessary steps to receive the benefits. Naturally, the details vary as the politicians write and rewrite the laws from year to year.

The first typical government entitlement comes in the form of a supplemental income check. Usually, these plans are called either Social Security (as in the United States and the United Kingdom) or Public Pensions (as in Canada and Germany). There is a formula to calculate how much per month each retiree receives. The amount varies based on such factors as number of years in the workforce, amount earned, and marital status. We need to contact the agency long before our retirement to obtain information on what we can expect to receive.

Most of these plans are funded through a pay-as-you-go system. Current workers pay into the pension plan and those funds are disbursed to retirees. The financial viability of such a system depends on the ratio of workers to retirees. In the future, given the current growth of an older population, either the workers will have to pay more or the retirees will have to receive less. These systems must continually alter their rules to stay solvent. Retirees need to monitor their countries' plans.

The second useful government program typically handles medical care. Following retirement, some or all of our medical costs may be covered. The most cumbersome of these plans is in the United States; it is called Medicare. Medicare has two categories: Part A and Part B. Part A, which covers part of the hospital care, is automatic; but Part B, which covers part of the doctor's costs, is optional. Medicare has lists of what percentage of what procedures it covers. There are many gaps. As a result, private insurance policies called "Medigap" are available. Retirees need to acquire the government information, study it, and act on their decisions (for example, enroll in Part B and/or buy a Medigap policy). Thus, they will know what to expect when medical attention is required.

Smaller programs that may benefit certain retirees include free or low-cost housing, food vouchers, and even nursing home assistance. Most of these offerings are targeted to lower-income people, often using a sliding scale or threshold points to determine eligibility. Additional assistance may be available for specific groups such as veterans.

It takes a bit of an effort, but all of us can navigate through the governmental maze to identify the retirement benefits that will assist us, our families, and our friends.

17 Allocate and Spend Money Wisely

The secret to relieving the fear of running out of money during our retirement is to spend a few hours reviewing past expenditures, determining what's necessary and what's merely nice, and then setting up a budget with the required expenses.

First, we must determine for which expenses we need to budget. This can be done by pulling out a couple of years' worth of checkbook registers and credit card statements and making a list of the various entries. For example, if we have a car, there will be gasoline, maintenance, and insurance expenses. If we have a house, there may be a mortgage payment, utilities, home repairs, home insurance, and property taxes. Other categories include clothing, groceries, entertainment, gifts, bank charges, doctors and medicines, health and life insurance, and other taxes.

After deciding on and coding the entries, we must add up the actual costs per year. If we pay cash for many items, such as groceries and toiletries, we may have to estimate what we've spent in these classifications. Continue this posting for a month or so, adding categories as needed.

Each of us decides what we want to track. With retirement, there may be some lifestyle changes. Perhaps we want to be debt free, paying off any mortgage and credit card balances. If we want to travel, we must allocate monies for various travel expenses.

Setting up our budgets gives us an awareness of where our money goes. Often, in the process, we decide we're not getting our money's worth out of some expenses. We cut back or eliminate these items. The trick is to become frugal without becoming cheap. We're frugal when we switch to a less expensive phone service that's easy to use and where transmission quality remains high. We're cheap when we buy a camera that costs little but makes out-of-focus photographs.

A computer with a personal finance program such as Quicken or Microsoft Money makes tracking our expenses much easier over time. Those without computers may purchase reasonably priced, preprinted forms such as the Dome Home Budget Book at office-supply or large discount stores. Or, we can devise our own systems. Once we have developed our budgets and adopted an expense-tracking system, it takes only a few minutes once a week to post our expenditures and keep everything on course. The resulting peace of mind is priceless.

18 Think Through Long-Term Needs

As we retire and age, our needs are not so different from other stages in our lives. Food, shelter, and clothing are our basic requirements. According to psychologist Abraham Maslow's hierarchy, other less tangible needs are to experience love, affection, and belonging; to nurture our self-esteem; and to achieve self-actualization.

We've had a lifetime of training and experiences to help us make new decisions. Our current challenge is to completely grasp our personal needs so we are not swept away in the flood of advertising messages aimed at retirees to trick us into purchasing items we may not need. Our finances form the foundation from which we meet our basic requirements and build our dreams and accomplishments. We must protect this financial foundation from unnecessary erosion.

With planning, our financial resources will continue to be adequate to meet our goals. Predicting our monetary needs is easier if we're not moving or making other big changes. For those organizing new ventures, some research provides educated estimates. It's advisable to try living on projected income (with projected expenses) for a couple of months in order to determine the accuracy of predictions and the appropriateness of plans. We can refine and make things work: budget and cut expenses, spend wisely, save and invest, and, if necessary, work to augment our income.

Avoid making home-equity loans (borrowing back what's been paid on the mortgage). Despite what television commercials promise, in most scenarios the loan reduces net worth and increases the likelihood of bank foreclosure.

Meanwhile, insurance companies have introduced expensive long-term-care policies (along with advertising and propaganda campaigns designed to convince us to buy them). If an individual can afford three years in a nursing home ($100,000 or more in liquid investments), he or she may not need such a policy. With high monthly premiums, few of us can comfortably afford long-term-care insurance.

But what if plans go awry? What if our mate is diagnosed with Alzheimer's disease? What if our home and possessions are destroyed by a tornado?

When faced with potentially draining emotional and financial challenges, we must attempt to find a new balance. Write down the quandaries and questions. Ask, How can I work through this problem? What are the obstacles? Learn to relax, shut out all distractions, concentrate, think broadly and creatively. Once our thoughts are organized and our plans broken into manageable steps, we can research our options, continue to perform desired endeavors, and feel good about our accomplishments.

19 Recalculate Insurance

Take a fresh look at insurance needs. What are the possibilities we need to insure for as we enter our retirement years?

If minor children are still living at home, we may need to continue carrying a term life insurance policy to provide for their care until adulthood. Term life is the least expensive life insurance as it builds no cash value. If we have no children or they are adults, we may elect to lower the amounts of our term insurance to pay for our funeral or cremation costs, and then help with any outstanding medical expenses or mortgage payoffs.

Another option is to act like an insurance company. If we have ordinary life insurance policies, we might redeem them. The cash value can be invested in bonds or stocks with good track records. Save the monthly insurance premiums, too. Then, on a monthly, quarterly, or annual basis, invest them. This means we become self-insured—and wealthier.

When the cost of health insurance began soaring in the late eighties, many Americans elected to take the risk of self-insurance. One couple refused to pay the latest premium increase; they began saving the monthly amount and crediting the account with money market interest. Twelve years later, their self-insurance account is worth approximately $45,000.

What this couple really likes about insuring themselves is that they are in control of what happens to them medically. No longer do they feel like members of the thundering herd who turn over control to the insurance company, doctor's office, or hospital by signing dotted lines. Health care providers suggest their treatment options, but the couple makes the decisions. In the past twelve years, the couple has sought treatment only a few times. They have become conscious of living a healthy lifestyle, taking charge of what they eat and how they exercise. They live much healthier lives than when they were insured!

This couple figures that their health self-insurance will take care of most scenarios. In the event of a car accident, their automobile insurance would help with medical expenses.

After talking with financial planners, this couple rejected purchasing long-term-care insurance, also. Only a small percentage of the population ever needs the long-term care covered by this insurance. When each qualifies for Medicare, he or she will purchase additional government coverage with Plan B. They will be very cautious about whether to select a Medigap policy. If they do, they will compare coverages and prices carefully. Meanwhile, they continue to invest into their health care savings. The account will continue to grow, allowing them to pay for the care they choose.

In the United States, insurance has become big business. We try to insure everything—even the weather on our vacations! Too often, we respond to the scare tactics of insurance sales campaigns and thereby overinsure. Each of us must look at our responsibilities, anticipate our insurance needs, research our options, and make intelligent decisions with which we feel comfortable.

20 Be a Savvy Consumer

Being a savvy consumer means obtaining what's best for us from the array of services and products available. This process involves being aware of changes in the marketplace and evaluating these changes to fit our personal needs.

For example, as the telecommunications industry grows exponentially, some of its new offerings may be desirable while others may only add frustration as we struggle to remember complex codes and procedures. Each option, such as cell phones, long-distance carriers, calling cards, call forwarding, call return, repeat dialing, or three-way calling, must be examined individually, its potential benefit weighed against its cost.

Changes are occurring in other sectors as well, such as finance, insurance, medicine, and entertainment. Read the fine print when notices and offers arrive with the bills. Some changes may be really useful. For example, one of the expanded benefits on a major credit card is a free message service while traveling!

In addition, thanks to telephone and Internet services, changes are happening in the way we shop. We let our fingers do the walking for the best prices and best rates. Handle these transactions with care, however, giving a credit card number to an unfamiliar business only when you're comfortable with the arrangements. When shopping on-line, make sure the padlock icon appears, indicating that the connection is secure.

Sometimes, being a savvy consumer means protecting ourselves from unwanted solicitations. As we become senior citizens with higher net worths, too often we're targeted for telemarketing scams such as opportunities to purchase gold, gems, and oil wells or to donate to a bogus charity. Make it a rule to just say "no" to *all* telemarketers. We gradually eliminate these aggravations in our daily lives by asking to be placed on the various companies' "Do Not Call" lists. In addition, we ask the Direct Marketing Association (DMA) to remove our names and phone numbers from all calling lists. Requests must be written and signed. Contact the DMA Telephone Preference Service at P.O. Box 9014, Farmingdale, NY 11725-9014.

Lots of unrequested offers arrive in the mailbox. Many of these offers can be stopped by sending a written and signed request to DMA Mail Preference Service, P.O. Box 9008,

Farmingdale, NY 11735-9008. Other ways to stem the flow of junk mail include calling the toll-free numbers on unrequested catalogs and asking to be deleted from the company's mailing list. Another tactic for dealing with junk mail is simply to throw away most pieces bearing bulk-mail indicia instead of first-class postage.

Remember, it's our phones, our computers, our mailboxes, our homes, our money, and our lives. Just because a salesperson calls us or knocks on our doors does not mean we have to spend our time talking with them. Just because a business sends us an offer does not mean we have to spend our time considering it or even opening it.

As retirees, we'll discover lots of real benefits, too. Many stores offer senior citizen discounts. Airlines, car rental agencies, and hotels often have senior rates. The National Park Service's Golden Eagle Pass provides free admission and half-price camping. Take advantage of these opportunities.

21 Save

Personal savings hold the key to a comfortable retirement. Most advice treats personal savings as only one of the three parts of retirement income. The other two are company pension plans and government plans such as Social Security. Since only personal savings are under our direct control, they may well be the most important.

A rule of thumb for all of us who desire financial security is to spend at least 10 percent less than we take in—living well below our means. This minimum 10 percent surplus can be put into savings. After we accumulate at least enough savings to maintain us for several months, we can invest subsequent savings using other instruments.

Retirement doesn't mean we stop this saving pattern. In fact, it provides the best cushion for unexpected future expenses, whether unscheduled dental work or a surprise trip for a grandchild.

When we look at the interest paid to us on our savings, we need to look at the net—how much we have after we pay taxes. If we receive 5 percent in interest and pay 25 percent of that interest as income tax, then the net interest rate is 3.75 percent. The easy way to calculate is to use $100. So, 5 percent of $100 is $5 and we must pay 25 percent of $5, or $1.25, as income tax. Now, consider the situation where inflation is growing at more than our net 3.75 percent rate. In effect, we are losing buying power with our savings. If inflation is lower than our net interest rate, we are gaining. This exercise illuminates why people look for the highest interest rates possible on their savings; they want their savings to grow (after considering both taxes and inflation). Certificates of deposit (CDs) and money market accounts typically pay a much higher rate than do regular bank savings accounts.

Often, we can take advantage of tax-free or tax-deferred savings plans. In the United States, such plans as 401(k), IRA, and Roth IRA offer tax advantages. One must begin withdrawing money from these accounts by age 70½. Putting money into municipal bonds provides tax-free income. Research available instruments and rates through banks and brokerage houses, or comparison shop on the Internet.

Pension plans are sometimes looked upon as a type of personal savings (forced upon us while we worked). Take time to get information on the pension plan and ensure the payout calculations are being done correctly. If a lump sum is received, we roll it over into an IRA to defer paying taxes on the whole amount. Taxes will be paid as amounts are withdrawn from the IRA.

Remember, savings are essential to a financially worry-free retirement. Start saving today.

22 Balance Investment Returns with Risk Factors

When saving for retirement and allocating funds after retirement, each of us faces a multitude of choices about where to put our money. We yearn for a high-yield, low-risk alternative—the perfect solution. Alas, we discover that no place is totally safe for our money. There are only varying degrees of risk.

Basically, we find two categories for our savings and investments. The first is lending—we let others have use of our money for their own purposes. In return for that use, they pay us interest. In the second category, purchasing, we buy items we think will increase in value—for example, stocks, real estate, and art.

We can be paid interest by financial institutions such as banks, credit unions, and brokerage houses (savings accounts, money markets, and CDs); by governments (notes, bills, mortgages, and bonds); by corporations (bonds); and by insurance companies (annuities). How much interest we receive will be determined first by how financially solid the borrowing institution is. (The more solid, the less interest we receive, but also the less risk that it may default.) Second, the longer we're willing to allow someone to use our money, the higher interest they'll pay. (A five-year CD generally pays more interest than a one-year CD.)

Since interest rates are typically not much higher than the inflation rate, many of us choose to invest in purchases that we later sell at a higher price. We are counting on this appreciation, or capital gain, being substantially more than the interest rate. Of course, there is the risk that the item may not go up in price. It could even come down. Historically, common stocks have been the most popular of this type of investment and the one with the best overall record. When we put our money into this alternative, we must understand that we're trying to predict the future. If we believe that this item will be worth more in five years than any reasonable alternative, we might buy it. If we give our money to a financial adviser or mutual fund manager, we are essentially saying that we agree with his or her prediction of the future.

Whether we lend money to receive interest or buy something for appreciation, we confront risks. We must determine how much risk we're willing to take. For a lower risk, we'll probably receive less interest or have less opportunity to see our purchases soar in value, but we may sleep better. What most advise is to diversify by spreading our money into several types of investments—some with low risk and others with a higher risk but a chance of a better return. For example, we may choose to put a large portion of our money into relatively safe interest-paying alternatives, a smaller chunk into the stock of solid corporations, and a tiny amount into high-flying, cutting-edge companies. This allocation would be considered a moderately low risk.

It's a good idea to make sure we completely understand the alternatives we are considering. Keep it simple. Also, we give high marks to instruments that are easy to sell and are inexpensive to buy and hold (minimum commissions and fees). Examples include blue-chip stocks bought and sold through discount brokers.

To make our decisions, we must first analyze our personal financial needs and how they are to be met. Then, we must predict what we think the economic pattern might be for the next several years. Finally, we must honestly confront how much risk we want to face. With these factors in mind, we pick the best blend of investment alternatives.

23 Know When Enough Is Enough

People with a great retirement have escaped the acquisitive mode. Garnering experiences has become more important than collecting stuff. Enjoying life has replaced the obsession with increasing net worth. This secret can be a difficult one to implement, however, due to conflicting messages in our society.

Once humans get started on any track of behavior, they become highly resistant to change. This tendency lies at the core of all addictions. Acquisitiveness is an addiction that affects most of the adult population in Western society. If a little is good, then a lot must be great. We want more. In our quiet, reflective moments, we know this compulsion rings hollow, but still we persist in the pursuit. When we feel momentarily uncomfortable in our choice of acquisitiveness, we call upon another human trait, rationalization. We say "we're saving for a rainy day," "this was a good buy," "the kids might use it," "we might need it," "everybody else has one," and so on. With a bit of effort, retirement is where all of this ends.

The trick to escaping the acquisitive mode is knowing how much is enough. What do we need for our daily lives? What do we need to follow our passions? How much must we have for our emergency plans? When we take the time to honestly answer these questions, we find that we require less than we thought. We may already have all we need.

When we feel out of control, a wonderful exercise is to buy enough food supplies for a couple of weeks and then escape to a remote, beautiful location without phones, newspapers, radio, television, and the like. Take books, hiking shoes, perhaps a canoe. Then, relax and live day-to-day. We are giving ourselves permission to enjoy ourselves and the natural world around us. When successful, this cold-turkey withdrawal from modern society opens us up to how little we really need to have some fantastic experiences.

Many people are tempted to accumulate more so that their estates will grow larger. Thus, the laudable drive to provide for young, helpless children continues well beyond the time it's needed. Our children are now adults with their own capabilities. How much do they need as a gift? Will it make their lives better or will it weaken their purpose? Will we be remembered only as a source of money? In retirement, we honestly face these questions and decide when enough is enough.

Since childhood, we've heard that money does not bring happiness. At this stage of our lives, we revisit that idea and apply it to our futures. We shift our focus from accumulating to living fully. We find there's much joy beyond the pursuit of more stuff.

24 Learn to Give

As we retire, generally, we enjoy our highest net worth. Over the years, as our salaries have increased, we've saved and invested. The trick now is to meet our long-term needs and to leave a legacy of which we're proud. To do this, we need to set up a realistic plan wherein we continue investing in our futures and giving to others.

Financial consultant Bill Staton takes his monthly income, deducts the amount he invests for himself and his family, sets aside the amount he wishes to donate to worthwhile projects, then spends the remainder on groceries, mortgage, utilities, clothing, transportation, and other monthly necessities.

Staton believes that people who mismanage their money use a different formula. These people concentrate on expenses. Instead of taking care of their futures and others first, they pay the butcher, the baker, and the automobile maker. Then, if there's any money left, they use it for their financial futures. The dilemma is that there's never any money left, because they haven't planned for any to be there! Consequently, there's no money to invest in themselves or give to others.

An astonishing element of giving is what we receive in the process. When we give wisely, we see positive results. We've made a difference. We feel better about ourselves.

Many believe that once we start giving, we'll actually receive more than we give. New Age author James Redfield, who wrote *The Celestine Prophecy,* notes that "No matter how tight money is for you, if you don't open your hand and make it available, it'll be hard for you to get more. When you give, you create a void that is filled again. And, you always receive much more."

In calculating how much money to give, some people allot 5 percent of their pretax income; others tithe 10 percent after taxes. Gifts can be made to individuals, community projects, or global endeavors. When giving money to family members, be clear about whether it's a gift or a loan. Experts caution that loans between family members are seldom repaid and that unequal gifts may cause resentments among family members.

With planning, each of us can give money. Often, though, what's more appreciated is giving time and effort, sharing expertise, or simply being available. Each of us has ways and means to help others.

When we give our time, effort, and money to others, we open ourselves to receive, too. Give from the heart. Help others feel good about themselves. To paraphrase John F. Kennedy, Ask not what others can give to us; ask what we can give to others.

25 Leave a Legacy

Retirement offers the perfect opportunity to reflect on our lives and ponder what kind of legacy we want to establish. A legacy is far more than a financial bequest. It also encompasses how we will be remembered.

Realize that we must have reached a certain maturity in our view of life to permit a contemplation of our legacy. It may be the first time we've ever put energy and resources into building for a future we may not see. Psychologist Erik Erikson calls this process "generativity." When we care about the younger generations, including our own children, we are exhibiting generativity. We look for relationships involving mentoring and nurturing. If we disdain this approach, Erikson warns, we will experience stagnation, being caught forever in a pattern of self-interest.

One of the most potent legacies available to everyone is to become an example for younger people. Think of the ideal qualities we've seen in an older generation. These characteristics might include happiness, spunk, humor, wisdom, acceptance, warmth, and perseverance. All of us tend to gravitate toward people who are loving, accepting, and considerate. By trying to exhibit more of these qualities each day, we leave a positive legacy that is priceless.

Consider how we would like our tangible assets to be disbursed. Much attention in the media revolves around estate planning to reduce taxes and increase the inheritance of our children. Understand that most of these articles are veiled advertisements by people with a vested interest—financial planners and attorneys who are trying to recruit our business. Instead, take a hard look at how much of our estates will be needed by our heirs. Much research and a lot of common sense indicate that there is a point where too large a gift does more harm than good. What's more, tax avoidance may not be worth an extraordinary effort, especially if we pay almost as much in professional fees as we save in taxes.

Let's investigate various alternatives for our assets and money. Consider giving some (or most) of it away while we are still alive. Small projects like landscaping a public building, setting aside land as a nature preserve, or funding a scholarship will enhance our feelings of well-being. There is even an option offered by at least one brokerage house (Charles Schwab) called a charitable gift account, whereby anyone can set up the equivalent of a private foundation. Investments grow tax-free; donations may be disbursed whenever there's a worthy opportunity. There are countless ways in which a well-timed and focused gift makes an enormous impact.

Most of us are not wealthy nor are we candidates for the Nobel Peace Prize. We can act as if we are, however, in order to leave a positive legacy.

26 Organize Legal Affairs

Retirement provides a no-more-excuses rationale for organizing our legal affairs. We can schedule an appointment with ourselves (and our partners) to put our records in order. Depending on our current systems (or lack of them), this work session could take anywhere from an hour to a couple of days. Here's a partial to-do list:

- List each family member with birth date and Social Security number.
- Identify locations of birth certificates, marriage licenses, divorce decrees, passports, vaccination records, powers of attorney, living wills, vehicle registrations and titles, and property deeds.
- Detail location of will plus name, address, and phone of the executor. Detail location of trust(s) plus name, address, and phone of the successor trustee(s).
- Inventory safe-deposit box contents. Provide location, names of owner and deputies, and instructions on how to access.
- List paid advisers (including addresses and phone numbers), such as stockbroker, tax preparer, accountant, life insurance agent, financial planner, and lawyer.
- Itemize income sources with phone numbers for contact.
- Enumerate bank accounts with account numbers and contacts.

- Name brokerage accounts plus any stock and bond holdings in our personal possession.
- Indicate employee savings, stock, or pension plans.
- Mention any other monetary accounts, such as children's trusts and grandchildren's education funds.
- Specify real-estate holdings with location of tax and mortgage records and deeds.
- List credit cards and loans with account numbers and contacts.
- Identify location of tax records.
- Record insurance policies with account numbers, limits, and contacts: life, health, and casualty.
- Designate funeral preferences and location of burial plot or columbarium.
- Detail any other important records.

Make at least two copies of this master list and store one away from home (in case of fire)—perhaps with our executors or successor trustees.

We're not finished yet. Make a list of all assets. This detailed inventory is especially useful for insurance purposes. A copy of this list needs to be kept somewhere other than our houses, also.

Next, we tackle any legal tasks we've been ignoring. For example, many of us want a medical power of attorney and a living will in place so we have a say in how we're handled medically if we become unable to communicate. Do-it-yourself forms are available in various publications and from the organization Choice in Dying (1-800-989-9455; www.choices.org).

Last, we need to check our wills. Are they up-to-date and consistent with our wishes? If not, we can use the advice, guides, and fill-in-the-blank forms contained in books and personal legal software. Many of us also find it useful to implement a living trust, which removes the time and fees of probate. Information on living trusts, and complete do-it-yourself packets, are also available in books and software programs. If our situation is particularly complex or our estates are worth more than a million dollars, we might want to involve a legal-financial expert.

While all of this paperwork appears less thrilling than following our bliss, it's a great feeling to have our affairs in order.

27 Know Legal Options

Retirement is a terrific opportunity to take more complete control over our legal affairs. In a hectic world, it is easy to turn to an expert such as a lawyer rather than learn to act for ourselves. For those who want to understand their options, there is more than ample legal information available.

We do our homework with magazine articles, self-help books, computer software programs, and Internet resources. With a computer, we update our wills and other legal documents such as advanced directives and trusts. We attend seminars and legal clinics. (Keep in mind, though, that some of these sessions may be marketing ploys for law offices.) We utilize resources available through senior citizen organizations such as the American Association of Retired Persons (AARP). The appropriate government agency may help for free. We contact our state departments of aging and our regional Social Security or Medicare offices. We do as much of our own legal work as we feel comfortable with and as the legal system will allow.

The basic challenge for all who reach retirement is to put our affairs "in order." Our first step is to create a record with names of institutions and contacts. On an annual basis, we need to update this information.

We arm ourselves with knowledge. We become aware of various scams. We create paper trails of our transactions (copies of everything coming and going). The more information we possess, the better our chances of obtaining what we want, with or without a lawyer.

If we need a lawyer, we compile a list of area lawyers who handle similar cases. Check with friends or businesses. Call to make an appointment to interview the most highly recommended ones. This interview ought to be free and the lawyer must be willing to come up with a written fee agreement. If not, keep looking.

In summary, to maintain personal control over our bodies, we must complete an advance directive. To ensure control over our asset distribution, we must prepare a will, establish a living trust, and transfer our assets to the trust. To handle other situations, we must increase our awareness and knowledge. In spite of the jargon and complexity of our legal system, with some common sense we can keep control of our affairs.

28 Lower Risk of Crime

Crime impacts retirees differently from the rest of the population. There's a lower incidence of violent crime, but a stronger likelihood we will be targets of financial scams.

Financial con artists are targeting retirees in record numbers. A recent FBI study revealed that 80 percent of the calls made by fraudulent telemarketers were aimed at older Americans. These criminals will attempt to grab our money through clever schemes that appeal to our greed, vanity, fears, or good nature. They contact us via telephone, e-mail, regular mail, and door-to-door calls.

One tip-off to a scam is the use of high-pressure tactics that require a quick decision. Also, most fraudulent operations will not provide detailed written information. Any unsolicited request for personal (Social Security number) or financial (bank account or credit card) information is probably a scam. Items that are "free" or business investments that claim "no risk" are highly suspect. We reject these solicitations. We take time to investigate our options before making a commitment to any purchase or investment. We tell telemarketers to put our names on a "Do Not Call" list.

Where we live and the places we frequent are the strongest predictors of our being the victims of violence. Metropolitan areas and marginal neighborhoods typically experience the highest crime rates. A low-turnover, neighborhood-watch community usually has the lowest risk. Regardless of where we live, there are steps we can take to lower our vulnerability.

To prevent pickpocketing and purse-snatching, the most likely attacks against seniors, we wear a waist purse or money belt, carry a whistle, and are especially alert when in crowded, unfamiliar territory. At our homes, other commonsense actions will lower appeal to burglars. They most often reject houses that are locked, watched, and appear to have someone at home. It takes little effort for our homes to meet these conditions. If we know thieves are after firearms, cash, credit cards, or jewelry, we remove those temptations. To avoid auto theft and carjacking, we avoid high-risk areas, lock our vehicles even while driving, and remove or disguise appealing items left in our cars. In all cases of potential theft, remember that our lives are more valuable than our stuff. Don't be foolhardy.

When we face the risk of crime realistically, the fears subside. One of the good parts of aging is that, statistically, we move into a lower-risk category. Yes, there are situations where we might become victims, but there are many actions we can take to lower that probability.

PART THREE

Develop Optimum Health

"I like the Chinese way of approaching health care. You pay the doctor when you remain well, not when you become sick. I've decided to stay as healthy as I can in order to avoid our sickness-based system."

RETIREE, AGED SIXTY-SEVEN

29 Get in Touch with the Body

Who is that in the mirror? Who is that person with the grandfather face or grandmother body, but who still has a young spirit inside?

Intellectually, we all know we're growing older. Emotionally, it's harder to admit because we may not feel any different. It seems we've only begun to be really comfortable in our skins, knowing our personal monthly rhythms and our tendencies regarding illnesses.

Just when we think we've got it all together, our bodies start changing on us. Our hair may gray, fall out, or grow in new places. Our eyes may need stronger glasses. Our skin may sag, spot, and wrinkle. Our posture and weight may change.

If our new appearances really bother us, there are things we can do to alleviate the distress. We could color, transplant, or electrolyze our hair; opt for laser surgery on our eyes; receive dermatological treatments for varicose veins, moles, and age spots; or have plastic surgery such as face lifts, breast lifts, and tummy tucks.

However, we can also choose to take pride in our years, our gray hairs, and our new looks. With a positive attitude, exercise, and a healthy diet, we can wear our new exteriors with grace and style.

Whatever we decide about our external looks, retirement is a time to pay more attention to our internal working parts as well. We need to know what's normal and what's not. When we experience an anomaly, we need to know where to turn for advice and treatment options. Find factual information on the Internet, in computer software, and in books. Consult with doctors, nurses, and pharmacists. Tap into the body's miraculous capacity to heal itself. Resolve to treat our bodies well by eating nutritious meals, drinking plenty of water, exercising daily, drinking alcohol moderately, and giving up smoking.

Taking care of our physical health benefits our minds, too. A study of aging people in Denmark, Great Britain, and the United States revealed that people who say their health is poor are more likely to feel lonely—even when they do not live alone!

We must refuse to beat ourselves up over conditions beyond our control. A recent MacArthur Foundation study indicates that maintaining a good attitude is more important than genes or luck in sustaining good health and achieving a long life.

Happily, it's never too late to improve our health habits. As one seventy-year-old marveled, "As long as I have my health, older is better than younger!"

30 Realize Intelligence Evolves with Age

There is no value in thinking of intelligence as a singular function that can be quantified by one number, intelligence quotient (IQ). Many separate abilities interact to create what we call intelligence. Each of us has relative strengths and weaknesses among these components, and our patterns change with age and experience. We may be better at creating a pun than visualizing a house from a blueprint drawing. We may have difficulty in remembering a joke but excel at solving a mystery. Every problem we encounter demands a different combination of mental skills. We use only a small portion of these abilities for day-to-day tasks.

During retirement, most people experience a switch in the roles they play and in the time they allot to various tasks. It's a glorious opportunity to exercise some of the intellectual abilities that may not have been used since school years. Current research suggests that those who stimulate different areas of their brains show the least symptoms of mental deterioration as they grow older. Arnold Scheibel, former director of the Brain Research Center at UCLA, says the brain is "wired to respond selectively to the new and exotic . . . We encourage people not only to remain active but to take up new pursuits." Dr. Scheibel reports that he takes his own advice—he and his wife are learning how to sculpt.

There is a small decline in the overall speed of mental processing as we age. We tend to slow down in the absorption of new information but we broaden in our capabilities to evaluate possibilities and produce answers, thanks to our lifetime of accumulated experiences. The decline in processing speed is slight—a fraction of a second when comparing a seventy-year-old with a thirty-year-old. Far too much attention has been paid to what is becoming weaker; our focus must be on developing strong new mental activity.

At some point, we may observe a disturbing loss of mental acuity in an acquaintance, a relative, or in ourselves. Before we assume that this condition is irreversible, look at the possible causes. The side effects of drugs and the interactions among them have an immense effect on mental processes. Emotional swings, poor nutrition (or absence of a crucial mineral), hormonal imbalance, and vision and hearing problems also have a negative impact on mental ability. Even if it appears that the person suffers from a type of senility, there are activities and procedures to help reduce its impact.

Additional mental stimulation shows quick and impressive results for all ages. We can learn a new language, play a different musical instrument, master a computer or another technical subject, or gain a skill (such as fixing a car or weaving a rug). The key concept is *new*. Using our mind in new ways is one of the most potent secrets for retirees.

31 Apply New, Positive Habits

Throughout life, as we watch ourselves and our acquaintances, it's easy to discern that humans truly are creatures of habit. Habitual actions appear to provide a sense of security, a feeling of being grounded, and a degree of pleasure. During our retirement years, we employ various habits—some old and familiar, others new to this phase of life. One secret to a great retirement is practicing habits that keep us mentally and physically healthy.

There is a mounting body of research that shows healthy habits applied at any age yield positive results. For example, in one study, strength training with ninety-year-olds in a nursing home produced increases in muscle size and strength, allowing several residents to walk without canes or walkers. Equally striking results occur when a healthy diet is employed and when individuals finally give up smoking. These benefits are available for free and for all ages.

The positive habits we need are an active daily life, regular exercise, a healthy diet, and plenty of mental stimulation. When we discover activities that satisfy these criteria, we repeat them until they become habitual. Once these good habits are in place, we're freed up to focus on the out-of-the-ordinary possibilities that will add even more zing to our lives.

For those of us with a long history of bad habits (or a lack of good ones), we may find retirement an ideal time to change. It's similar to adopting New Year's resolutions. The trick is to change deliberately, with plenty of self-congratulatory messages. Guilt is to be avoided. Rather, we must give ourselves credit for each behavior we change. If we walk for fifteen minutes today, we think of how good this is rather than tell ourselves that we should have walked for forty-five minutes. If we're changing our diets, we focus on one meal at a time rather than dwell on our overindulgences.

Ideas that may help us change our routines include associating with people who have healthy habits, graphing changes, taking photos (before, during, and after), and calculating savings (for example, less money spent on alcohol, cigarettes, and associated medical problems). Rewards give incentive, too. If we've exercised daily, eat out at a health-food restaurant. If we've given up smoking for three months, take a mini-trip. Celebrate our new healthy habits!

Maintaining our healthy regime must remain a top priority. As Somerset Maugham said, "The unfortunate thing about this world is that the good habits are much easier to give up than the bad ones."

32 Practice Preventive Medicine

Retirement brings higher awareness of our bodies—their changing and eventual demise. Unless we're wearing blinders, we see what's happening to people older than ourselves. Research the common problems and current methods for prevention and treatment. With this knowledge, we can modify our lifestyles, diets, and habits.

In the past century, health officials focused on adding years to our lives. They were successful: in the year 2000, the average American enjoys twenty-five more years than did the average American in 1900. The United States Public Health Service has adopted a new series of objectives to improve the nation's health into the next century. One of these goals is to improve each adult's functional life, primarily by educating the public about smoking, exercise, and nutrition.

Learning and adopting the practice of preventive medicine pays off. We feel better; we spend less on medical problems.

To reduce the likelihood of cancers, heart attacks, and a host of other illnesses, we give up smoking. The health benefits begin immediately when we quit the habit, no matter how long we've been smoking. In addition, we're more pleasant to be around. We cough less, and we smell better.

To decrease the risk of heart attack and stroke, we engage in regular aerobic exercise. Also, we take an aspirin a day, if our doctors concur. To help prevent osteoporosis, diminish the likelihood of falls, and lessen arthritis pain, we engage in strength training (both resistance exercises and weights). In addition, we take 1000–1500 milligrams of oyster shell calcium (with vitamin D to aid absorption) to keep bones strong, lowering the risk of osteoporosis and broken bones.

A healthy diet is a must in maintaining a high degree of body function. Each of us must know our tendencies and plan nutritious meals accordingly. For example, if we gain weight easily, the American Dietetic Association recommends we look for ways to lower fat intake. If we have high cholesterol, we must take in more protein and fewer carbohydrates, according to Mary Eades, M.D., and Michael Eades, M.D., authors of *Protein Power*. If we're sensitive to insulin, the American Diabetes Association instructs us to avoid sugars. Vegetarian or omnivore, we want plenty of vegetables for all their fiber, vitamins, minerals, and bioflavonoids.

Roy Walford, M.D., author of *How to Double Your Vital Years* and *The 120-Year Diet*, suggests that as our bodies become less efficient, we take vitamin and mineral amounts far higher than the Food and Drug Administration's guidelines. If we can't ingest these quantities through our daily diets, we may take a multivitamin. Look for purity and fair pricing in a multivitamin that includes vitamins A, B_6, B_{12}, C, D, E, and K, and has beta carotene, biotin, calcium, chromium, copper, folic acid, magnesium, manganese, molybdenum, niacin, pantothenic acid, riboflavin, selenium, thiamin, and zinc. Many multivitamins are formulated especially for mature adults.

According to most longevity experts, additional supplements may be a good idea, too. Saw palmetto reduces the size of men's prostate glands, relieving pressure on the bladder and, consequently, raising activity and sleep levels. Coenzyme Q10 has helped many people increase their energy. If insomnia has become a problem, try taking melatonin every night before going to bed. Research recommended daily allowances. Start with the smallest amounts and evaluate the results. As always, consult a doctor.

A food that all of us can consider adding to our diet is green tea. Drinking one cup a day lowers the risk of cancer, according to nutritionists.

The goal is to maintain the highest possible levels of body function for as long as possible. Get smart and practice preventive medicine.

33 Pay Attention to Diet

Today's food consumer has more choices and more variety available than ever before in human history. We have fresh ingredients year-round. With such an abundance of healthy foods, we may wonder why the rates for obesity, adult-onset diabetes, and other food-related maladies have soared over the past twenty years. Sadly, it has to do with us not taking charge of what we choose to ingest.

During retirement, we want to eat healthily and well. We improve the variety and nutrition in our diets. We relish the complete dining process.

Let's choose to prepare our own food and to do it with gusto. For those who've been too busy or have never learned to cook, now is the time to begin. Basically, anyone who reads can learn to cook. We find a wealth of cookbooks at our public library and local bookstore, and most night schools and adult centers offer cooking classes. Let our imaginations run wild. For example, try nothing but new recipes for one month straight. When holding a dinner party or covered-dish event, have everyone agree to prepare dishes no one has ever tried before. Couples may divide chores such as chopping and combining. Each person could develop their own specialties. Make cooking fun.

When we decide to eat out, let's make it a special occasion. Find restaurants that prepare unusual combinations that may give ideas for future personal recipes. Or choose restaurants that prepare dishes that are too cumbersome to try at home. Retirement is a perfect time to swear off those fast-food and unexciting chain restaurants, whose predictable dishes often rank as the least healthy.

For special physical needs, we alter our diets to improve our health. If high blood pressure is a problem, research shows that foods such as salmon will help reduce it. For high cholesterol, ask the doctor about implementing a high-protein diet as a healthy alternative to medication. Persons with chronically high cholesterol and triglyceride (another blood fat) levels experience a drop to normal within weeks of starting a high-protein diet. As more and more studies are performed on foods and their interactions, we are discovering that a well-planned diet accounts for a large part of our health and well-being.

Our bodies respond to the foods we feed them. Let's make retirement a feast worth remembering.

34 Stay Active

Retirement can bring excitement or it can lead to lethargy. We determine the activity level.

Staying active is more than getting out of bed in the morning. It's getting off the sofa, too. It's attending social, cultural, and religious events. It's going to a party, seeing a ballet, or attending church. It's getting our hair cut. It's going shopping. It's mingling with others and taking care of ourselves as much as possible.

When we stop and think about it, there are lots of little ways that each of us can increase our activity level every day. While talking on the phone, we stand or walk around. While the morning coffee brews, we tidy the house. While watching television, we never lie down; instead, we sit and perform simple activities such as mending or knitting to burn more calories. Even better, we get out of the house. We go shopping, attend a meeting, or play bridge.

All the acts we perform while lying down, sitting, standing, walking, or driving a car could be evaluated. Which ones can we change to give ourselves a boost? While sitting in front of the computer, we could schedule a five-minute break after every twenty-five minutes. We'll find ourselves physically and mentally refreshed. If we're taking regular walks, we could add variations. Today we walk faster; tomorrow we climb hills. If we're having trouble with motivation, we could enlist a buddy. If we have the choice of an elevator, escalator, or stairs, we could opt for the stairs. When shopping, we could park farther from the store entrance and walk. If we have an errand less than a half mile from home, perhaps we could walk instead of drive.

Check our schedules. How much time is being spent inside the house? Can we alter our routines to go out more frequently? Analyze our diets. Could we eat lighter meals or drink less alcohol?

Ask ourselves what other habits may be making us sluggish. Are we smoking? Are we taking medication? Can this be changed?

In addition, staying active means stimulating our minds. It's more than reading the newspaper, listening to the radio, and watching television. It's working the crossword puzzles, taking part in radio call-in shows, and selectively watching television programs in order to participate later in conversations and group discussions. It's interacting with others and helping solve the world's problems.

Look into the future. What do we see—a slug? A bore? Perhaps it's time to make conscious efforts to stay active.

35 Exercise

While staying active entails maintaining a high function level, exercising means adopting physical fitness routines to tone the body and mind. The benefits of exercising are astounding, making all efforts worthwhile.

It has been shown in study after study that workouts increase the physical capabilities of people at every age. A classic 1960s study examined a group of seventy-year-old men completing a one-year exercise program. At the end of the study, these men were in the same physical condition as the average forty-year-old man. These men ended the year with the physical reactions of the average man thirty years younger! A 1990s study of ninety-plus-year-olds placed in an exercise program found that they more than doubled their strength, improved their balance, and greatly increased their walking ability.

If we still need convincing, examine recent research on the positive effects of exercise. A 1998 MacArthur Foundation study cites dozens of projects. The research shows that between exercisers and sedentary people, the exercisers sleep better; have less chance of gallstones, colon cancer, diverticular disease, heart disease, diabetes, osteoporosis, and enlarged prostates; experience less pain from arthritis; and have less anxiety, lower blood pressure, and fewer falls. Basically, fitness cuts our risk of dying. This is a compelling reason to exercise.

To stay supple, stretch. Stretching exercises can be done in bed upon waking. First, we raise our hands over our heads and extend our legs. Point and flex the hands and feet repeatedly. Next, we pull our knees toward our chests and raise our heads toward our knees to make a ball. Hold this position for as long as possible, working toward thirty seconds.

Take a thirty-minute walk at least four times a week. One may vary the walks or select a smooth course such as a track. The faster the walk, the better the workout for feet, legs, lungs, and heart.

Other workouts include dancing, jogging, bicycling, skating, rowing, swimming, water aerobics, bowling, baseball, basketball, tennis, golf, calisthenics, weight training, martial arts, and yoga. Some exercises develop aerobic capacity (such as jogging) while others increase strength and endurance (such as weight training). Still others improve flexibility and balance (such as yoga or martial arts).

The trick is to find a mix of enjoyable physical activities that fit into our daily schedules. Exercise is so important that it may be time to consider structuring our day around the workout. If it helps, join a health club.

Studies have shown that the best exercisers are those who have a ready alternative if they can't do the primary exercise. If it's raining, they work out with a video. If their partners are not available, they have a plan B.

Some exercises can be done while doing other things. For example, we can perform squats, ankle circles, leg raises, or side bends while watching television, talking on the telephone, or waiting for a pot to boil.

When we retire, it's time to become more vigorous. Among other benefits, exercise gives us more energy and helps us focus. Exercise may be the simplest and most important activity that affects our quality of life. Just do it!

36 Avoid Hazardous Products and Situations

Healthy retirees tend to avoid unhealthy situations. It's a simple secret, but one most of us fail to consider in our hectic lives.

Consider implementing three simple steps: avoid all cigarette smoke, drink alcohol only in moderation, and always use a vehicle's safety belts. No other common habit in our culture has a more negative health impact than smoking cigarettes. There are one hundred times more people dying from the legal use of cigarettes than the combined deaths caused by cocaine, heroin, and other illegal drugs. Moderate use of alcohol, especially red wine, may be healthy. Heavy use, like the regular cocktail hour, however, may lead to both physical and social problems. Too often, retirees turn to alcohol to kill time; the results are disastrous. Fastening seat belts is the simplest preventive task we can employ. Taking this action would prevent half of all traffic fatalities.

To reduce our risk of cancer, we implement a healthy diet and cut our exposure to radiation and cancer-causing agents. Together with tobacco avoidance, these actions, according to some researchers, would prevent almost two-thirds of all cancers. Keep X rays to a minimum. Use protective clothing and lotions to minimize the effects of ultraviolet rays. Reduce or eliminate use of chemicals and pesticides. Stay up-to-date on the latest cancer-prevention research.

Our environment may not be as safe as we would like. Investigate the air and water quality of the area. If we have allergies, take a hard look at the amount of pollen or mold. If we cannot remedy the situation, we can always consider a move.

As we and our friends age, take action to prevent accidents. When toddlers are around, we make adjustments to "childproof" the house. Similarly, as we become less surefooted ourselves, we slipproof all stairs and rugs, install handles and rails as needed, and place items within easy reach.

When driving, we need to monitor our changing bodies. Depth perception will become poorer; reaction times will become slower. We exercise our privilege to drive safely by minimizing noise within the vehicle and concentrating. Be more alert when backing up, turning, or switching lanes.

Prevention is thinking ahead. Let's vow to improve our chances of a healthy retirement by practicing prevention daily.

37 Learn What to Do in Emergencies

Arming ourselves with skills and knowledge about possible emergencies is one of those tasks that's easy to delay until it's too late. Yet, when we take the time to get ready, we feel more confident and secure.

Retirement brings a higher probability that we or someone near us will need emergency help. When we were younger, we might have been faced with a sports injury or appendicitis; in retirement, it's more likely to be a heart attack or stroke. No matter what age, we may experience accident, fire, or storm dangers.

One essential step we can take is to become certified, or renew our certification, in cardiopulmonary resuscitation (CPR). The course is offered in most communities, usually sponsored by the American Red Cross. In addition, it's an excellent idea to take a basic first-aid course or study a book on first-aid procedures.

Learn how to answer questions such as, What can we do if someone appears to be having a heart attack? In this case, the answer is to give the person two aspirin and immediately seek medical help. According to the Center for Cardiovascular Education's *Heart Attack Guide*, the aspirin significantly raises the chances for recovery.

Warning signs are crucial for seeking timely medical help. For example, an impending stroke is often forewarned by what is termed a transient ischemic attack (TIA). The symptoms are a sudden loss or dimming of vision, an unusual numbness or weakness in an extremity or in the face (especially on one side), unexpected speech difficulties or mental confusion, sudden severe headache, or unusual unsteadiness in standing or walking marked by dizziness or falls. When these symptoms appear in combination, the probability of a stroke is raised. By knowing our medical histories (and those of the people close to us), we can identify other conditions we may want to study so we know the warning signs.

There are simple measures we can take around our homes to increase our chances of survival. Test all smoke alarms on a given date, such as a birthday, every year. Most retirees who die in fires either do not own a smoke alarm or have a malfunctioning one. Never smoke in bed. Know all possible escape routes, in case of fire. Hold a home fire drill. Similarly, rehearse storm or earthquake emergency procedures. In addition, ensure that both our kitchens and our vehicles are equipped with fire extinguishers and first-aid kits.

It's impossible to become an expert in every possible emergency. We look at the odds, however, and prepare ourselves to deal with those most likely to occur. It's a comforting feeling to be ready.

38 Know Options for Medical Treatment

One of the top concerns for most retirees is how to obtain high-quality medical care. This challenge is made more difficult when we relocate or travel extensively during our retirement years.

Often, we'll get a preview of our own dilemma as we assist our parents or older friends with their medical decisions. In the health care arena, the secret to success is to take charge, think broadly, and evaluate all options.

Acute needs such as massive injury, heart attacks, strokes, or the sudden onset of disease require immediate, quality care. Investigate local options before they are needed. For the more common chronic conditions, we can be more selective with our decisions.

Our bodies belong to us, and we're in charge of what happens to them. The first opinion is our own. If we need a second opinion, we might turn to a friend, nurse, doctor, herbalist, computer program, book, or folklore. There is seldom one remedy; everybody has an opinion. The healthiest retirees appear to be those who choose their second-opinion providers well, but never shortchange their own thinking. Research on longevity shows that people with minimal contact with the medical system live the longest.

If we have a condition that requires advice from someone else, be prepared. During the evaluation, attempt to understand not only what is happening but why. Insist on a dialogue rather than submit to a lecture. Remember that most conditions are related to diet and lifestyle—two areas that are under our control. When the body's balance is disturbed, subtle changes to our diets or habits may work as well as or better than harsher actions such as medications or surgery. We must remind our medical professionals of our preferences.

Our task is to understand the possible courses of treatment. If medication is suggested, we need details. What is the brand name? What is the generic name? How does it work? What are the alternatives? What about a change in diet and exercise? How and how often should medication be taken? What should we feel, and when will we feel it? What are the side effects? How does it interact with other drugs and foods? When can we discontinue it? What is the research that supports our taking it? In other words, we want to know what we're putting into our bodies.

If an invasive treatment such as surgery is suggested, we want even more information. Why is the body not performing well? What are the risks from having or not having the surgery? How will surgery provide correction? Will any function be lost or any imbalance created? What would life be like without surgery, as opposed to life with surgery? What are the alternatives? Will additional surgery be required? What are the odds of complications? What is the medical profession's success record? What is the doctor's win-loss record?

Look for options beyond pills or surgery. Many medical professionals are now incorporating more varied alternatives for treatment. Investigate how the condition is treated (and how successfully) in countries around the world. For example, several retirees found that simple back exercises developed by a New Zealand clinic obviated the need for surgery. While there's probably no perfect solution, we can amass options that will help us make better decisions.

39 Discern Between Viable Choices and Hoaxes

One constant through the years has been the prevalence of snake-oil salesmen. All of us desire to feel healthy and look good. Thus, we search for the magic pill and the fountain of youth. If we naively believed all advertised claims, we could take certain drugs and vitamins, rub on a few salves, incorporate a few exercises, and live forever. How do we separate the valuable techniques from the useless or destructive ones? How do we join the successful retirees who have lots of energy and few discomforts?

Many of the claims touted by various companies are grossly exaggerated. Over the years, we've been exposed to enough marketing gimmicks to realize this. Still, there's the lure for a quick end to arthritis pain; Americans spend more than $1 billion every year chasing that dream. We spend countless more on diet pills to magically erase pounds. We spend billions on prescription drugs that may be ineffective—even harmful.

We need to know what's behind the information we're receiving. If what we hear or read is being put out by the producing company, we must be skeptical. We want nonprejudiced evaluations. We understand that in this fast-paced world, harried doctors' sole source of prescription drug information may be from drug-company salespeople. Look for independent research and reviews. The Internet provides several medical sites with complete drug information; many libraries carry the *Physicians' Desk Reference*.

The more potent the option, the more cautious we need to be. Keep in mind a phrase from the Hippocratic oath: "First do no harm." A sobering lesson comes from the findings of a 1990 U.S. Inspector General report. People over age sixty accounted for over half of those hospitalized for drug-related problems. This group was four times more likely to die from effects of prescribed drugs than any younger group. Among annually reported cases of dementia and accidental falls, over 50,000 were caused by improper medication. The more drugs taken, the greater the danger.

Let's look afresh at eating a healthy diet, taking a few supplements, exercising regularly, lowering our stress levels, and staying happy. This regimen is free, does no harm, and models the style of the most successful of those who have preceded us on the retirement road.

40 Prepare Medical Directives

Like legal affairs, medical directives are easy to put off. We all know we're going to die, but, being human, we postpone preparing for death. However, once we execute a living will and/or durable power of attorney, we enjoy knowing that we've helped prepare our partners, our families, and our trusted friends for our death. Once the discussions and paperwork are complete, it's as if a huge burden is lifted from our shoulders. We no longer have these chronic, nagging thoughts about what we need to do. We've done our best.

Since the inception of Medicare, Medigap, and Medicaid, American medical establishments have turned dying into a profitable business. The majority of an individual's lifelong medical expenses will be incurred during the last six months of life. Too often, people are shuttled from one expensive test, procedure, or treatment to another with little knowledge of or input into what's going on.

We can take more control over our medical affairs. First, we need to put together the puzzles of our various health insurances. We must understand what our personal health insurance policy covers and what it does not, and we need to know when government programs begin to assist. Do we need to purchase additional insurance? Once we understand how the systems work, the answer is often no.

Next, we need to know which legal directives are appropriate for our situation. If we want some say in how we die, we need to execute a living will. Use a preprinted form or simply write out what we want and do not want in the event of incapacitation. The organization Choice in Dying offers forms that can be ordered by phone (1-800-989-WILL) or downloaded from its Website (www.choices.org). Libraries and bookstores carry guides, too. The form needs to be tailored to the state in which we live. If traveling, we may need to carry more than one type of form to meet various criteria such as the number of witnesses.

Another advance directive is called a durable power of attorney. It appoints someone to serve as a health care representative (or proxy) in the event of incapacitation. This person does not have to be a family member, just someone we trust to make life-and-death decisions for us.

For a person to make such powerful decisions, a lot has to be discussed. For example, where do we want to die—at home with hospice care? In a nursing home? In a hospital? How do we feel about organ donation? Among potential medical treatments such as pain medications, blood transfusions, chemotherapy, radiation, and experimental procedures, which are acceptable and which are not? Which life-sustaining programs can be implemented? If heroic measures are taken, when would we want "the plug" pulled?

Talking about death makes it less frightening. Together, we and our significant others face medical options. We talk about practicalities and personal preferences. Usually, this becomes a modeling and sharing process, helping others tend to their medical and legal plans, too.

PART FOUR

Build Emotional Strength

"*Retirement is the perfect time for reflection. And, when I reflect, I realize how foolish many of my emotional states have been. I'm more aware and more in control now than in those earlier times when I thought I knew everything.*"

RETIREE, AGED SEVENTY

41 Regulate Emotional States to Enhance Health and Life Span

More and more data accumulate to suggest that the most important variable for predicting our long-term health is how well we handle our emotional state. In *The Attitude Factor*, Thomas Blakeslee reports that happy, well-regulated individuals with poor physical habits can have healthier lives than those with positive physical habits but negative emotional situations. This finding clarifies why some centenarians have reached their ripe old age in spite of bad habits. Of course, the best strategy is to take care of both our bodies and our minds.

We need to be alert to the dangers of denying our own emotional needs, concentrating on unobtainable goals, or always trying to fulfill the expectations of others. These learnable (and unlearnable) conditions strongly affect our immune systems and, consequently, our life spans.

For our overall health, we need to be aware of our basic emotions and to continually adjust our behavior. We seek long-term pleasure and well-being. We must eliminate or alter what appears to be a hopeless situation. We must avoid denying our feelings or continuing with routines that create feelings of hopelessness. Achieving long-term pleasure and well-being requires action. Often, we remain locked in destructive behaviors because we fear the short-term pain of changing the status quo. If we take the risk, we enhance our lives.

To change our ways, think about different approaches to modifying our behavior. In the case of a negative situation, try to alter it, avoid it (or certain people), or change our attitude about it so it isn't as disturbing. Visualize ourselves trying each of the alternatives and imagine what might happen with each one. Finally, select the most promising option to try, and learn from how well it works or doesn't work. Continue this experimentation until we've improved our emotional state. Simple steps lead to powerful results.

Regardless of our past histories, we can learn to unteach ourselves and try something new. When things go wrong, we don't have to let our emotions follow. Nor do we have to accept bad feelings as inevitable. With a bit of effort on our part, we discover the power of being happier, more loving, and more in control of our emotions. We may even live longer and healthier in the process.

42 Learn to Live Happily

Happiness is more than a feeling; it's a choice. Many of us may wonder how an elusive state of mind can be a choice.

It may be helpful to look at what people think keeps them from being happy. We tell ourselves that we inherited a predisposition. We were trained to postpone happiness. We've procrastinated about forming our philosophy of life. We have no focus, purpose, or passion. We're comparing ourselves to others. We're fantasizing. We've made happiness conditional on certain events or on others' behaviors. We've confused happiness with success and, even, with fun. We feel unworthy or guilty. We're victims. We're voracious. We've forgotten how to show appreciation and give gratitude. We erect all kinds of hurdles to happiness—perhaps because it may be easier to be unhappy than happy.

As we read through that list again, we see that happiness pays no attention to age, success, wealth, or education. Circumstances do not cause an individual's happiness or unhappiness. It is determined by people's reactions to actions or events.

So, how can one learn to react in a happy way? First of all, throw the idea that one *should* be happy out the window. However, we do want to work on accepting ourselves, building satisfying relationships, searching for meaningful activities, and maintaining an open attitude. We want to enjoy life, finding our core pleasures, having new experiences, and seeking actualization. There are many ways to do this—some insignificant, some momentous, many common.

We can be as enthusiastic as we decide to be. We may be happy at any place, at any time. It's how we choose to view the experience that makes the difference. We can opt for delight and ecstasy or we can choose despair and misery. To help us along the way, listen to the teachings of therapists such as Barry Kaufman (*Happiness Is a Choice*) and Dennis Prager (*Happiness Is a Serious Problem*). Kaufman's one-step program is simplicity itself—decide to be happier starting today.

As we retire and make changes in our everyday lives, learning to be happy may be one of the most important. Start this instant. Choose happiness.

43 Develop a Positive Attitude and Open Mind

As retirees, it's important to realize that we can have a dramatic impact on how successfully we age. As we grow older, our environment is more important than our genes. Basically, if we've lived to sixty-five years of age, we've overcome our inherited weaknesses. What's important now is the strength of our attitude and our openness to the world around us.

Most personality traits, such as emotionality, shyness, and impulsiveness, are influenced by heredity. A classic study at Pennsylvania State University analyzed 350 sets of Swedish twins over age sixty who were raised in separate homes. The results revealed two personality factors that are not affected by heredity—attitude and agreeableness. Each of us can control our attitude about what happens in our lives. Each of us can become more agreeable in our relations with others.

- How do we go about boosting our attitude and good nature?
- We approach the future with a sense of adventure. What have we always wanted to do in our lives? What have we yet to experience? Who is there to meet? What can we learn?
- We practice being positive. We say "yes" whenever possible, especially to new activities. We let go of being judgmental. Being critical can be destructive to ourselves and our relationships.
- We stay engaged. We enhance our days with fresh flowers, special foods, or favorite musical recordings. We plan something we want to do weekly to stimulate our minds. We create long-term goals and make plans to meet them.
- We nurture ourselves, enjoying our experiences and feelings. We smile and laugh! We spend time with other happy people. We appreciate nature.
- We adopt healthy physical and mental habits. Keeping our bodies and minds vigorous helps us achieve higher mental and physical capacities.
- By harnessing our powers and believing in ourselves, we become more productive. In the process, we improve our health, enhance our attitude and congeniality, and, consequently, enjoy more satisfying lives.

We can change at any age. In retirement, let's seize this opportunity to improve our attitude and agreeableness.

44 Show Appreciation and Gratitude

Retirees have much to say about appreciating and being grateful for their lives. Listen:

"I've realized it's not enough to have a wonderful life. I must acknowledge it and be grateful for it."

"I look for what's good and true in my life right now. Constantly, I'm expressing my gratitude and appreciation."

"I try to regularly express appreciation and spontaneously convey gratitude."

"I'm glad for every day."

"We can feel gratitude anywhere, anytime. We make it real by expressing it to others."

"I start every morning by thinking of someone to thank. It can be anybody: family members, friends, acquaintances—past or present. It can be God. Expressing gratitude gives me an inner peace."

"Saying grace, giving thanks—all that keeps me from taking all the good things in my life for granted."

"When I stop and think about what I'm grateful for, one image after another pops into my head. It's the various people who've influenced my life in some way. It's my children. It's my health. It's my independence. My list goes on and on. Whenever I have the chance, I try to express my appreciation."

"Often, being able to spontaneously express appreciation to people will not only make their days, it can influence their lives."

"It's interesting that no one is ever so important or so busy that he or she doesn't enjoy a genuine compliment."

"Anyone can afford to be generous with appreciation and gratitude to others. They are available to everybody, not just the wealthy."

"I think expressing gratitude is a mark of a generous spirit. It shows sensitivity to others, too. It's something almost all of us can improve upon. It's kind of like regularly practicing those random acts of kindness and senseless acts of beauty. It's all good stuff!"

"Sometimes I'm too shy to say what I think, so I try to put my thoughts on paper. Either way works for me. Interestingly, it seems the more good thoughts I give, the more I receive."

Let's appreciate our retirements and be grateful!

45 Challenge Irrational Beliefs

Who is in charge of our emotional state? We are! Our beliefs about the world around us create our moods. When those beliefs are rational, our emotions are well regulated and generally positive. When those beliefs become irrational, we experience devastating consequences such as extreme stress, depression, hostility, or rage. Irrational beliefs also lead us into immature behavior such as blaming others, procrastination, or avoidance.

We can challenge and change our irrational beliefs. The reward for doing so is great—a healthier, happier emotional state. Whenever we find ourselves experiencing an intense negative emotion such as strong anxiety, anger, or depression, we need to stop and analyze our beliefs. We may find that we're fretting over events we cannot change; that we're upset because we believed someone should not have acted the way they did ("should"s and "shouldn't"s are almost always irrational); or that we're expecting others to be looking after us and solving our problems.

Fight the irrational beliefs. It's a common tendency for us to overgeneralize ("the youth of today are terrible") or to polarize ("she has an absolutely perfect daughter"). We can worsen every unpleasant event into a catastrophe. We might overpersonalize our worlds ("only I should win the lottery") or expect others to read our minds ("they should have known what I needed"). We may blame other people and events for our predicaments, when in actuality the way other people act toward us is largely a reaction to our own behavior. Perhaps we tend to avoid `difficult situations rather than face them. We may replay an irrational belief or relive a negative event over and over. In short, our irrational beliefs can control our lives unless we fight them at every turn.

In our retirement, we do not have to be perfect. We do not always have to be in control. We may have fears. While there are no guarantees in this world, we do not have to obsess about our security. We can choose to be more rational, starting now.

Life's problems are real. What we seek are mature, workable methods to deal with them. Demonstrating humor and altruism, finding substitutes and alternatives, delaying our immediate gratification, gaining perspective, and taking a new course of action help us cope without entertaining irrational beliefs and the subsequent negative emotions. Let's not waste time worrying about things we can't change. Rather, let's focus on what we can improve—our personal belief system.

With rational beliefs, a catastrophe becomes merely a frustration or disappointment; other peoples' behaviors are seen as understandable rather than horrible; our predicaments are viewed not as someone else's fault but as a problem for us to solve. Irrational beliefs leave us in an emotional muddle; rational beliefs provide a sane disposition and a course of action.

46 Recognize Brainwashing

The number of retirees increases daily, and the marketplace is reacting. We are seeing not only a frenzy of senior-directed marketing, but also a more sophisticated targeting of messages using gender, wealth, and educational status. Amid all this noise, the happiest seniors will be those who have learned to listen to their own inner voices.

Most information that comes into our lives is aimed at trying to change our behavior. Someone else wants us to take an action that will benefit him or her. Advertising leads the pack with messages extolling products and services that supposedly will improve our existence. Drug companies tout magic pills that will cure all of our physical ailments. Insurance companies soft-sell fear to work on our insecurities. Using similar tactics, politicians, television evangelists, and radio hosts appeal for our support and minds. The barrage continues twenty-four hours a day. We face the difficult task of separating meaningful information from half-truths and distortions. Even the most discerning individuals may be duped.

It helps to understand some common techniques used to push ideas. One of the most popular and effective devices tries to convince us that we can be part of an "in" group or one of the "good guys" as opposed to the bad and undesirable "them." Testimonials may be offered, glittering generalities bandied about, even name-calling thrown in. The approach could use the "just plain folks" angle or it might include symbols such as a flag or a cross to heighten credibility. Often, logical fallacies abound. To further encourage us, there may be a push to "get on the bandwagon." Or, the message might try to work on our fears and uncertainties. All of these gimmicks are part of the propagandist's toolbox.

We need to arm ourselves with several questions: "Who does this benefit?" "Why would they be using this technique?" "What is the source (the authority) for the information?" If we hear or read an "expert" opinion, we must ask, "Who's paying this expert's salary?" Recognize that repetition doesn't make something true. A valuable defense is to strip away all the emotion and glitz surrounding a message and analyze it as we would a contract. Be a bit cynical and dubious. Let the issue sit for several days and then look at it again in a calmer emotional state.

Those who best resist brainwashing and propaganda techniques are those with a strong sense of identity and understanding of where they are heading in life. With that center and some hardheaded questioning, we are able to better determine our retirement future instead of feeling lost without a compass.

47 Practice Relaxation Techniques

Why is relaxation a big secret of retirement? All of us know how to relax, right? Perhaps not. There's an immense difference between effective relaxation and taking a nap or kicking back and watching a movie. Relaxation involves a person concentrating so well that blood pressure lowers, the heart rate slows, soothing alpha brain waves increase, and a sense of well-being floods the body. As the stress releases, good feelings intensify. People who engage in regular meditation improve both their mental and physical health.

From birth, some of us have more of a tendency toward tension than others. We readily see differences in temperament among small children. Among adults, we hear of type A personalities and their tendency toward heart attacks. We vividly recall our own moments of tension, anger, and high stress. We've all experienced that edge, the times when we've been acutely uncomfortable, almost out of control. The good news is that even if we tend toward a high-stress, high-tension profile, we can dramatically lower those sensations with relaxation techniques.

Relaxation techniques have many names: meditation, yoga, self-hypnosis, breathing exercises, martial arts, sensitivity training, prayer, massage, or communing with nature. The underlying component of all of these is the individual's inward focus into a calming state. Let's take a simple example, breathing. We all know how to breathe; it's automatic. When we focus on the breath, however, we begin to sense a change. We feel the breath; we shut out distractions. Slowly, we change our physiology for the better. All relaxation techniques help us achieve a more calm, centered state of being.

With regular practice, relaxation dramatically improves our lives and our health. It's used by athletes to enhance their performance. It's used by the devout to feel closer to their religion. It's used by the fearful to release their fears. It can be used by all to simply feel better and more in control of their day-to-day lives.

Take time during retirement to explore several of these relaxation techniques. Check for course offerings or instructional tapes. Favorites will soon emerge. Then, with regular practice, feel the difference.

48 Face Fears

As Franklin Delano Roosevelt said, "The only thing we have to fear is fear itself." In retirement, our fears can take control of our lives—but only if we allow them to do so.

As we retire and age, we may frequently feel that our well-being is under attack. Our physical appearance and energy levels are changing. We might be unable to continue performing a favorite activity. We could be experiencing a persistent pain. A disease could be threatening our physical health. Our eyesight and hearing may have diminished. We might be feeling unproductive. We may be grieving. Loneliness could be affecting our mental health. Money concerns can become an obsession.

We hear ourselves asking, "If I move, will I adapt?" "If my spouse dies, will I be able to take care of myself?" "Will I become a burden to my relatives?" "Will my money last?"

If we want a great retirement, we know it's important to feel good about ourselves and in control of our lives. We must face our fears in a rational manner. We use the strengths, experiences, and wisdom of ourselves and others to help us meet the challenges of this stage in our lives. We research subjects of concern. We attend motivational talks and seminars. We talk to friends and family members. With all the ideas we collect, we make our own plans. In the process, we find that our fears lessen.

We keep ourselves adaptable by continuing to try new things. Giving up a talent we can no longer perform does not prohibit us from developing different capabilities, such as gardening. We prepare to take care of ourselves by mastering skills we lack. For example, men may learn to cook and women may acquire home and automotive maintenance skills. New methods and ideas help maintain high levels of mental function.

It's important to continue contributing to our families, friends, communities, and society. Our experiences provide much-needed wisdom and empathy. New friends keep us learning fresh ideas. Younger friends help renew and inspire us.

The fear of running out of money can be allayed by planning. Evaluate income and expenses. Develop a budget that covers needs and allows occasional frivolity. Develop an emergency fallback plan to use if money becomes tight.

If we find ourselves despairing over a situation, we need to realize that it's a sign of strength to ask for help. Beyond family and friends, we might take advantage of community resources for counseling, transportation, housing assistance, medical services, and legal and financial advice. Reaching out to solve a specific problem does not mean becoming helpless.

In retirement, it's important to accept the realities of aging and death. Denying them only makes it harder to find our answers and solutions. Throughout our retirement, we can adopt an attitude of continuing to grow and being a life force.

49 Accept Death

Few individuals in our society grow up discussing death as they do other topics such as love, friendship, and marriage. That situation changes with age. We encounter the deaths of family members and friends—at first, those of the older generation, but soon our contemporaries. The more experiences we have with the deaths of others, the more likely we'll eventually take a hard look at our own future. We can learn from successful retirees who appear to have come to an understanding about mortality.

As with other concepts, death becomes easier to handle if it's not hidden under a list of forbidden topics. The essential step is acceptance. It seems so obvious, since death is one of the few sure things in our lives. Amazingly, many act as if they are going to dodge this inevitability. We desperately search for a supplement, exercise, or spiritual encounter that will not just enrich our lives, but give us immortality. Many cultures throughout history have suggested we live every day as if death is close at hand; some visualize it as a bird on our shoulder. One retiree shares, "I live every day as if I have a terminal illness."

Once we accept the inevitability on an emotional level, we reshape our priorities on how we want to live each day. We begin to use our lives in more meaningful ways.

Regardless of our beliefs about the possibility of an afterlife, we realize that part of us will live on as memories within those close to us. That is a living legacy for each of us. The acceptance of death allows us to focus on the type of memories we want to bequeath. How do we want to be remembered?

Also, once we face our eventual demise, we are able to make arrangements. We might choose our epitaphs, write our obituaries, decide on cremation or burial, and write out our preferences for any service or party.

Does all this talk of death seem morbid? Perhaps we prefer Somerset Maugham's tongue-in-cheek approach: "Death is a very dull, dreary affair, and my advice to you is to have nothing whatever to do with it." Our wishes notwithstanding, death will come for us. So, let's make our retirements as good as they can be.

50 Understand the Process of Grief

How is understanding the grief process a secret to retirement? In our retirement years, we will encounter death more frequently. It's useful to know what to expect and what to do for ourselves and for others.

When we lose someone we care about deeply, we must give ourselves permission to grieve. Although it's human nature to avoid dealing with pain, it's healthier for our psyches to deal with the loss when it happens. Not grieving at the appropriate time may be likened to not cleaning a wound; infection may set in.

We must allow the grief process to take as long as we need. At the time of the loss, we feel numb and detached. It is as if we're living in a state between life and death. We are experiencing a change, an ending to life as we knew it. In this dormant state of mind, it may take a while to find meaning in life again.

Sometimes people may not fully understand the magnitude of a loss. They'll mouth such phrases as, "Time heals all wounds." The passage of time will certainly help, but what's more beneficial to healing the wound is what we *do* to celebrate and honor the person we've lost. For example, we can look at photos and put together an album. We can listen to and sing "our song." We can watch his or her favorite television show or movie. We can prepare a remembered meal. We can visit a place special to that person and talk to him or her. We can write letters to the individual. We can keep a journal about our feelings. We can compose poems or songs about our relationships.

Hopefully, these activities will bring tears to our eyes. Tears are the body's way of releasing strong emotion. Tears will allow us to let go of our anguish.

We'll experience all kinds of feelings as we mourn. We'll ask, "Why?" We'll deny the reality. We'll try to bargain. We'll feel angry, abandoned, depressed, empty, anxious, listless, relieved, and regretful. We may feel as if we're going crazy. We may lose our appetites. We may be unable to sleep. All of these feelings and behaviors are normal reactions to loss.

It's reassuring to read articles and books as well as to listen to friends' and families' insights about the grief process. It may be even more beneficial to attend a support group where we share our stories and hear others' accounts. Such a group helps us verbalize our feelings and realize that others are experiencing the same muddle of emotions.

As we progress, we'll come to an acceptance of the death and be able to let go of our loved ones. There will be many little signals that we're healing. We may be willing to make and carry out plans with friends and relatives. We may decide to take care of a pet. We may feel capable of assisting someone else. During this time, we'll develop a new relationship with the individual we lost—one that exists in our hearts and minds. We'll incorporate what was good in this person into our own lives.

If we get stuck along the way, feeling angry or victimized, there are mental-health professionals who can help us reach new understandings. Seeking such counseling is a constructive choice, not only for ourselves but for others around us.

We know we have actively worked through our grief when we acknowledge that our lives have changed, and that we're now open to what's yet to be.

PART FIVE

Seek Vital Relationships

"Whether you're single or in a relationship, these retirement years are a heap more fun with lots of acquaintances and a few good friends."

RETIREE, AGED SEVENTY-ONE

51 Express Love and Kindness

When seniors are asked for their tips to a great retirement, the majority of the comments have to do with expressing love and kindness. As we age, we learn the value of loving and caring for friends and relatives and, in turn, being loved and cared for by others. Here are a few of the seniors' comments:

"The best advice I can give anyone is: Be kind."

"Showing kindness is more important than being perfect or being right."

"I like to practice those random acts of kindness."

"I'm happiest when I'm nice to others and unhappiest when I'm not."

"It doesn't cost anything to be nice."

"Nice guys usually finish first in other people's books."

"Be generous with kind words, smiles, hugs, and kisses."

"Demonstrate tenderness and affection."

"Reach out and touch someone every day. People love that human touch—pats on the arm or back, hugs, and kisses."

"Every day I try to tell someone what I like about him or her."

"Always leave loved ones with loving words. It could be the last time you see them."

"Never go to bed on an unsettled argument."

"Give love as an adult but take it unconditionally like a child."

"Show compassion toward others."

"Love as much as you can—more quantity and quality, toward people and things."

"The more love you give, the more love you receive."

"Love is a great investment. It returns great dividends."

"To love and be loved is the greatest joy in the world."

Why so many comments about sharing love and kindness?

As we age, we become more in touch with what's basic, real, and important in our lives. Obviously, all of us like to love and be loved. It's exhilarating. We also enjoy being kind to others; it makes us feel more lovable. We feel safe and secure when we feel loved. These are basic human needs and emotions.

Although we feel we will live longer and have opportunities to express our love and kindness to those we care about, we often come to realize that we may not have more time. Now that we are older and wiser, we must seize the day—now—and show our love.

52 Seek Out Other Happy People

This is a simple secret to enjoying our retirement years: no matter where we find ourselves, seek out other happy people! We may be in our hometown, we may be traveling, or we may be in a retirement center. Wherever we are, we determine our happiness to a great degree by recognizing specific behaviors that make other people, including ourselves, happier or unhappier.

All of us want to miss "organ recitals" that give blow-by-blow accounts of medical problems. We want to bypass "nonfiction least-sellers" describing past career or stock market triumphs. We want to escape endless "historical novels" enumerating family members. We want to elude "soap operas" reciting who did what to whom. These are examples of ego-centered pontifications, dealing with one person's body, past achievements, money situations, family members, and acquaintances.

In addition, we want to circumvent judgmental comments that criticize everyone and everything. We want to shun the fearful predictions of gloom and doom. These pronouncements never enrich anyone's life. They simply make people feel upset or scared. We don't like these behaviors in others; thus, we don't want to exhibit these behaviors ourselves.

Instead of getting caught up in these irritating behaviors, let us look to inspire others. If we smile, will others smile? If we're cheerful, will others respond accordingly? If we show a sincere interest in others, will they reciprocate? If we let go of our judgments and our fears, will we enjoy more positive experiences with other people? The answer to all these questions is yes. Humans are sociable animals. We like to be around other people—especially happy people.

To increase our happiness, we avoid people we've identified as egocentric and boring or critical and fearful. Instead, we seek out people who are other-directed, interesting, and optimistic. We apply behaviors that we know people will respond to in a positive way. And, of course, smile! Simply by smiling, we create a lot of happiness.

53 Become a Better Listener

Improving our listening skills at any time of our lives would benefit most of us. Especially during retirement, however, we must resist the tendency to ramble on and on about how things used to be while shutting off meaningful dialogue with other people. For a great retirement, choose to become more like the thoughtful, wise seer who others desire to be around. One of the crucial components of that model is being an excellent listener.

The first technique in being a better listener is to be fully present when someone else is talking. That means all of our concentration is on the other person and on what he or she is saying at the moment—not on previous conversations or extraneous events. It may be hard to be fully present with a family member with whom old noncommunicative habits have built up or with someone who is not our favorite companion.

The next technique is to accept all feelings and opinions without passing harsh judgments. This skill appears to go against our very nature. Whenever we hear something, we almost instinctively label it as correct, crazy, dumb, wild, or wonderful. We instantly judge rather than fully hear the message. This tendency is especially evident when the communication involves strong feelings or sensitive ideas. To completely understand someone, we may have to alter our own beliefs a bit to accommodate the individual, and that's not always easy.

Too often during the listening process, we respond with advice or opinions. If we continue listening nonjudgmentally for a while, these temptations will subside.

The most effective listener is an active one. An active listener serves as a mirror to the talker, reflecting back what the listener thinks was said. This reflection gives the talker a chance to amplify or clarify what was meant. In this clarification process, it's amazing how often we discover that we partially misunderstood what the talker was trying to say. Active listening prevents a lot of negative emotional reactions.

Other workable responses include asking someone his or her opinion and then actively listening to the response. Or, ask someone for help—with an idea, a specific action, or a social dilemma. Almost everyone responds enthusiastically to these approaches.

When we choose to work at developing these better listening skills, showing more patience and complete understanding, we'll discover greatly improved interpersonal relationships.

54 Improve Existing Friendships

How does one go about improving existing friendships? The first thing to do is think about our friends. They may be friends from school or even preschool years, or from an old neighborhood or hometown. They may be friends we met through business, church, the military, an organization, or our children's activities. They may be friends who were introduced to us by other friends. They may be friends we've made on a trip.

Next, think about why these individuals became friends and why other people didn't. Usually, there were commonalities. In our early years, similar age and shared experiences played strong roles in our selection of friends. As we matured, our interests developed and our friends changed.

If we still cherish those good times we had with "old friends" with whom we may have lost touch, we may be able to track them down through records kept by schools, churches, towns, and the armed forces. We may be able to find listings in phone books. (The Internet contains phone books from many countries.) We may be able to renew acquaintances at a reunion or celebration. We may reconnect, rekindling mutually satisfying relationships.

Long-distance friendships can be maintained through phone calls, e-mails, cards, and letters. Share articles, cartoons, or jokes that may appeal to the other person. Many friendships can be sustained with once-a-year holiday greeting cards and letters.

Newer friends may live nearby. These relationships can be improved by consistently showing a constructive interest: making phone calls; stopping by for a chat; inviting them for a walk, a meal, a movie, or any other event they would enjoy. Listen to their problems. Look for ways to show interest and concern. It's caring. It's sharing—our lives and theirs!

To stay in touch with friends takes commitment to others. Being a friend means giving emotional support, love, and admiration as well as information and practical assistance. When we receive the same, we know we have good friends.

55 Make New Friends

Whenever we make a significant transition—graduating from school, getting married or divorced, having children, switching jobs, moving our home—we face an upheaval in our circle of friends. Retirement creates a similar disruption. If we relocate during retirement, the change becomes even more dramatic. To have a great retirement, as one senior put it, is to "never lose your enthusiasm for meeting new people and seeing new places."

The ideal situation during retirement would be to have companions and friends who could provide stimulation, acceptance, intimacy, emotional support, and practical assistance. In difficult situations, we may find that the best support comes from those who have experienced similar challenges. But more now than at any other time in our lives, it becomes important to reach out beyond those who are like ourselves. Creating friendships with all age groups is one of the strongest recommendations from successful retirees. This process will require more effort if we are living in an age-segregated community.

When we select our activities carefully, we will come in contact with lots of new people of all ages. One retiree chose to volunteer as a campground host at a national forest, another to staff an art gallery, yet another to work with youth groups. From taking classes to joining an athletic club, we find enjoyable endeavors that will allow us to make new acquaintances. We look for commonalities in the people we meet. We seek opportunities to mentor younger individuals or a couple. Take one retiree's advice:

"You have to go beyond the initial impression. I've found lots of interesting stories hidden beneath the surface."

To enhance our own "friendliness quotient," stay abreast of topics that are useful in conversation. Learn to practice more acceptance and less judgment. Offer to help without expecting a payback. Talk less and listen more. This type of investment in developing and maintaining new friendships will yield substantial returns during our retirement years.

56 Enjoy Sex

Disregard our society's attempt to equate sexuality with youth. In 1999, AARP commissioned a study on sex, which showed that a fulfilling sex life greatly enriches the lives of older people and their partners. With the gifts of time and experience, the sexual act can be more varied and rewarding than when we were younger.

Since we are no longer likely to procreate, one has to wonder why there is still a desire for sex. It's basic: humans like to feel turned on. The thrill of excitement does not disappear with age. In Eastern cultures, the energy associated with achievement is often called creative, sexual, or spiritual energy. Freud called it the libido. Whatever we call this energy, it feels good. We may sublimate it or deflect it from the usual sexual outlets, but we seek it because of its positive charge.

If we enter retirement as part of a couple, there is no better time for reestablishing or strengthening our intimacy and communication. Talk about what drew us together, what special qualities we like in the other, and what we find sexually interesting. Vary our daily routines to decrease stress and increase times for closeness. Make our sex lives a priority. Seek treatment for any interfering physical problems. This may be a good time to buy a new manual on sex. Try out new positions. Act out scenarios. Become the best sexual partners we can be.

The odds are strong that we will find ourselves without a partner at some point during retirement. This situation is even more likely for women. Being single does not mean being sex-less. The sexual mores that have evolved over the years focus on providing a stable environment for raising children. With our new increase in longevity, especially for women, the old mores do not work nearly as well. If we find ourselves without a partner, be aware of all the possibilities for affection. We do not have to blindly follow an arbitrary or outdated path.

Aging presents its own set of problems associated with the physical aspects of sex. Male impotence, also known as erectile dysfunction syndrome (EDS), can be treated with drugs, herbs, surgery, counseling, or a combination. Both men and women benefit from doing Kegel exercises daily. These exercises strengthen the muscles in the pelvic area. Most of us can be fully capable of enjoying orgasmic experiences into our eighties and beyond.

Sexual energy may not be the most important component of our lives. It does, however, offer us great pleasure and emotional benefits.

57 Enrich the Marriage

The morning after our retirement parties, we still wake up next to the person we've been waking up with for so many years. Today, however, feels different. It's the first day of the rest of our lives together.

The first year of retirement can be a real challenge for married couples. The "I don't have to work anymore" inertia can carry over into marriage, creating boredom. Of course, conflicts and challenges will arise. Two people who were busy with other roles are suddenly thrust together twenty-four hours a day. In this new, unstructured circumstance, power plays develop around the smallest things. Tension is created if one takes over what the other is doing or complains about the quality of the other's performance. For example, *he* wants to learn to become a gourmet cook in *her* kitchen while *she* wants to turn *his* lawn into a perennial flower garden.

Even though we may have been married for years, we discover we still have to work at our marriages. We must remember and celebrate what attracted us to the other person in the first place. If disagreements happen, we need to give each other space. There will be other times when we enjoy being together. Focus on these more positive moments.

Planning and discussing will help us find solutions to any recurring problems. The first few weeks and months of retirement are the best time to reexamine who does what, and to make accommodations for each other's likes and dislikes. One simple, effective way to head off problems is to talk every morning at breakfast about what we would like to do that day, including what we might want to eat for lunch and dinner. Then, as we set out on our various tasks, individually or together, we know we are on a mutually agreeable track.

With the additional time together, there are more opportunities to enjoy romance and intimacy. Take time to focus on each other, whether it's at home, at a restaurant, at a party, or on vacation.

The relationship must continue to adapt to the changing influences of health and money. In one common scenario, the woman wants more sex while the man feels less "up to it." Another is when one person becomes a hoarder of money while the other wants to spend. As these changes occur, we must make every effort to understand and accommodate our partners' feelings. We must be honest about our own feelings, too. If we have

trouble finding solutions and communicating our feelings, however, there are counselors who can help.

With a positive, loving attitude, there are lots of opportunities to enrich our marriages and our lives. Remember the good
times enjoyed together. Focus on what we do well together.
Compliment one another. Listen to and show enthusiasm for
each other's ideas and wishes. Get excited about each other all
over again.

58 Support Our Partners in Achieving Personal Dreams and Pleasures

Retirement presents many couples with the biggest problem in
their relationships. The radical changes in tasks, goals, and time
allocations can disrupt even the most placid partnership. To forge
a great retirement, both individuals must make the effort to find
creative solutions.

Perhaps the most common pattern is when one partner has
finally retired from a job that has been constraining. He or she
has made few plans other than to take a major trip or spend lots
of hours in a favorite leisure activity. The partner is barely considered. After the first few months, boredom and strife arise.

Another possibility is where a stay-at-home partner finds that
upon the other's retirement, he or she wants to branch out. These
new work, volunteer, or social goals often play havoc with the former roles that were developed in preretirement days.

How can each partner feel fulfilled without feeling abandoned? How can each become the other's strongest supporter?
Disgruntled comments like, "Oh, he's probably out playing golf
again," or "She must be off doing one of her volunteer bits" do
not indicate a strong, supportive relationship. We need to balance. The most successful couples do this as an ongoing process,
ensuring that neither feels deserted, stymied, or trapped.

Both of us must communicate our dreams, what we would like to achieve, and how much change we're willing to attempt. Then, we work on merging our goals. It will require some acceptance of the other's ideas, integrated with our own. We'll have to decide what will be separate and what will be joint endeavors. In the best scenario, we discover new ways to share.

There are innumerable possibilities for a new synthesis. Perhaps one person wants to photograph nature. The partner could assist (by providing technical help or simply carrying equipment), enjoy another hobby such as hiking while on outdoor shoots, or pursue totally separate entertainments. With a positive solution, neither will feel useless or out of touch. Perhaps one has an opportunity to take a position (volunteer or paid) that fulfills several personal goals. Both partners explore whether the other can help in this pursuit or is better off with separate activities that fill the time. Always search for the solution where both partners feel like winners.

One of life's great rewards is in seeing someone we care about achieve a dream. In retirement, we may have that opportunity. We can work with our partners to achieve new bliss.

59 Adjust the Role of Parenting

Those of us who are parents will discover that finding a workable parenting model has an immense influence on the quality of our retirement. It can be the best of times—adult-to-adult conversations, sharing positive moments together, developing strong family bonds—or the worst of times—experiences marked by guilt, blame, financial dependency, alienation, and frustration. We must realize that although we can't control our adult children, we can control ourselves.

Act in ways that foster stronger relationships. Share memories of special moments with our children. Let's face it: most of us never tire of hearing someone talk about us in a positive way, and that holds true for our children, too. Remember the good, funny, and poignant times when they were growing up. Find old photos and other mementos to make the memories more tangible.

Another way to strengthen ties is to give of ourselves. Help with chores or special home improvement tasks is generally a welcome gift, especially for busy children. And, working on a project together may be very rewarding. Baby-sitting gives young parents a break. Assistance with decorating, gardening, or financial planning can be appreciated, if our children have asked for our help. No one appreciates unsolicited advice.

As we learn, make decisions, and adjust our lives to retirement, we discuss the process with our children. They benefit by seeing us as still growing, while we benefit by not being seen as dull and boring.

Financial help within families can be like walking through a minefield. Do we feel for our children and grandchildren, or are we trying to control them? If they stay dependent, will they begin to exhibit a welfare syndrome? What if they want to move back home because of illness or loss of job? The issues are thorny, and there are no ready-made answers. We must remember that our children are adults and must deal with their own problems. Bailing them out may not always be the best choice. Whenever we do become involved financially, listen to the experts and ensure that a written agreement is put into place, just as a bank would do. Find additional advice in books and from other retirees, accountants, and support organizations.

We must try to avoid the all-too-familiar parental themes: criticizing our children's decisions; pleading for their sympathies by using guilt; favoring or talking about one child in front of another; or blaming problems on someone else. Instead, we might vow to develop an adult-to-adult relationship as we would with a new friend.

Finally, we seek to stave off what can be a horrific issue for families: "What are we going to do about Mom and Dad?" Early

in our retirement, we talk with our children about our preferences for when our health becomes an issue. While we're still
physically and mentally alert, we need to let our wishes be known
in case we need future help and support. By delaying this discussion, we are avoiding our responsibilities and putting the burden on our children.

The lawyer Clarence Darrow once jokingly remarked, "The
first half of our lives is ruined by our parents and the second half
by our children." Let's do better for ourselves in the second half.

60 Understand the Role of Grandparenting

We may have become grandparents before retiring. What's different now is that without work, there are more opportunities to
enjoy our grandchildren.

Just as there is no single, right way to parent, there is more
than one way to grandparent. There are many different styles;
what's important is creating strong relationships that both we and
the grandchildren enjoy. Not being the primary caretakers, we
can simply be supportive of our children and have fun with our
grandchildren.

We can act crazy about each grandchild. It's fun for us and
it's great for the child's self-esteem. Being there as often as possible, we play, teach, and encourage. Grandchildren love for us
to listen to them. We listen to their meaningless chatter as well
as learn their favorite toys, clothes, television shows, movies,
music, and sports. We must grow as they grow. Often, during the
school years, we provide a much-needed balance to the demands
of academic and extracurricular activities.

It's important to support our children's passage into par-
enthood, too. As they learn to parent, we learn how effective
our own parenting skills have been. We help mediate conflicts,

helping cushion the realities of life for both our children and grandchildren.

Thinking of our children and grandchildren as our successors, we carry on traditions and recount family history. There are favorite vacation places, holiday practices, recipes, and photographs to share.

If grandparenting from afar, make tapes of riddles, jokes, stories, and books. Carry on an oral tradition by passing along family history. The grandchildren might love stories from their parents' and our own childhoods, especially the funny ones. Put together scrapbooks or videotapes that they can look at anytime. Call often. When the grandchild is old enough, encourage them to call collect. Of course, we visit as frequently as possible. In between, we send letters that include surprises such as cartoons, stickers, and sticks of gum.

Give our grandchildren our unconditional time and energy. In return, we'll receive their unconditional love and respect.

61 Help Parents and Other Older People

As we approach and pass into retirement, we become more aware of the conditions facing our parents and other older acquaintances. Perhaps we are looking at our own not-too-distant future. Our behavior could be considered an application of the golden rule: help others as we might wish to be helped.

Due to the increase in life spans, we find the average woman spending as many or more years assisting in the care of one or both of her parents as she did in caring for her children. (The trend affects males, too, but their average life spans are shorter.) The caregiver role can be very difficult—especially if it involves caring for someone who seemed invincible at an earlier stage in our lives. We may find, however, that our involvement strengthens our own emotional development.

When assisting older people, our first challenge is to comprehend what they are going through. We must avoid "old-age" stereotypes. Each person will have a unique pattern of diminishing capacity. He or she may have a financial challenge, feel a loss of purpose, experience physical difficulties, or be grieving. These are challenges they face, not hopeless obstacles.

We provide positive expectations that they will adapt to each stage of the aging process. We help them implement a pattern of good diet, exercise, minimal drug dependency, and an active mental life. Often, simple assistance goes a long way toward making their lives (and ours) more fulfilling.

There will be times when we must find additional help for an older person. There are many options. Only a small percentage of the elderly live in institutions. Many seniors live alone with specific outside help as needed. Become aware of the senior services that are available in the community. Shared living (where a friend or family member shares space, expenses, and chores) works for many. This option does require a clear delineation of the arrangement and duties—particularly if it involves family. Retirement communities, ranging from elder apartments to full-service facilities called continuing care retirement centers, may provide meals, housekeeping services, social opportunities, and even medical help. A nursing home might be the last resort as many rely heavily on medications and offer the least stimulation to the patient. There are, however, significant differences among homes. If this option is necessary, investigate to choose the best available.

When considering alternatives for additional help, all of those concerned must be involved with the decision. Too often, we might be tempted to bypass other family members or even the elderly person himself. Working toward a consensus is well worth the effort. The older person may take a bit longer to process and accept any change. Recognize that there are negative effects from inertia and inaction. Making no decision *is* a decision—often the worst one.

Working with older people, especially our parents, can be a marvelous bonding time. It can offer serious challenges, also. We do best when we allow ourselves full empathy—putting ourselves in their shoes.

62 Give Up the Myth of the Happy Family

There are as many perceptions of family as there are individuals. People's experiences range from abused to smothered with love. Thank goodness, there is a lot of room between these extremes for more normal family relations.

What is a normal family? What is the purpose of family? When answering these questions, we must first realize that human societies have encouraged the family unit of a father, mother, and children for the purpose of raising children to be responsible members of the tribe of man. Throughout human history, the extended family of aunts, uncles, and other older, wiser adults has played a strong role in this maturation process. Today's society, with its highly mobile population, has created smaller family units. A high divorce rate accentuates this trend. Thus, we understand that what was considered a normal family in the past is not considered a normal family now. Furthermore, what is deemed a normal family in one part of the world may not be regarded as such in another. Still, many of us cling to a one-dimensional Norman Rockwell image of a family.

Another factor in family dynamics is the shift in roles and responsibilities over time. As a child grows and becomes more independent, parents must let go. Adult children must find a more mature way of interacting with their parents.

Many family problems arise because individuals do not change as their roles change. A father or mother may try to continue to control. A son or daughter may try to be taken care of long after

SEEK VITAL RELATIONSHIPS

the necessity has passed. A sibling who has always picked on a brother or sister may continue that behavior into adulthood instead of treating the other as a grown-up. Sometimes these difficult family members create terrific disturbances in our lives.

In the best of all worlds, family members would accept and love each other unconditionally. In real life, however, it simply does not work that way. For our own emotional health, we must recognize that the concept of the happy family is a fantasy. What we must deal with is reality. We must carefully examine our own behavior within the family dynamic and strive for a rational, mature stance.

During retirement, we consciously decide whether to spend more or less time with family members. Either way, we give our best efforts to accept and love each individual. We maintain contact. We talk to each other by phone (if not in person), attend family celebrations, exchange notes and photos. We can be the first to ask for forgiveness for any wrong, even if it's imagined. Let go of guilt. We cannot change others, but we can put forth our best personal efforts.

63 Be the First to Forgive

With retirement comes time to remedy things in our lives. We no longer have the reason, or excuse, that we're so involved in our work that we have little or no time for others.

As we contemplate what we've achieved and what we still want to accomplish, it's a good time to remember people who helped us along our way. Where are they now? Can we pick up the phone or write a note to express our appreciation?

Who were the people who held us back or placed stumbling blocks along the path? Why did they act that way? Were we infringing on an area they regarded as theirs? Were they jealous of our success? Until we place ourselves in their shoes and really try to understand, we'll never know. Can we forgive these people for what they knowingly or unknowingly did to (or didn't do for) us? In our minds, we let go of the hurts. We forgive. If these people are still alive and we know where they are, we call or write a conciliatory note. They may wish to resolve differences, too. It may have been only pride that's kept everyone feeling offended and alienated. On the other hand, these individuals may not respond in a positive way. They may not have reached their own new understandings. It's important to hold on to our new awareness of ourselves and others.

We may need to forgive ourselves, too. Perhaps there are things we feel we should or should not have done. Maybe we wanted to accomplish more in our work or an area of interest. Is it too late to improve any of these situations?

Retirement is a time when we can obtain an even bigger picture of life and grow with our perceptions. It's a time to let go of little and big things such as misunderstandings, distressing events, even pipe dreams. Instead of waiting for others to forgive us, ask for their forgiveness. Instead of pursuing what's impossible, reconcile with ourselves.

Come to grips with these issues from our past. Find a way to accept ourselves and others. In the process, we enjoy peace.

64 Bond Again

For those of us entering retirement as part of a relationship, we need to recognize that there's a strong possibility we will become single again. In fact, the likelihood is at its highest point in our lives. Estrangement, divorce, and death become significant agents of change during this last part of our lives. After age sixty-five, less than 40 percent of the women live with a spouse; by age eighty-five, that number drops to 20 percent.

When we find ourselves single, perhaps for the first time in many years, we face a significant challenge. One of the strongest reasons for initially creating a marriage is to provide a base to raise a family. That reason is no longer pertinent for retirees. The desire to bond again may come instead from loneliness, social pressure, financial need, or infatuation. If we become single, we may notice a change in roles, status, and relationships with family, friends, and community. Couples often socialize exclusively with other couples. A single often faces a barrier with former friends.

The secret to a satisfying bond requires us first to feel good about ourselves. This simple notion is incredibly difficult to achieve after a divorce or death. It takes time and work on our part, but a successful new relationship is unlikely to occur if we haven't reached a positive plateau. Second, we must grasp what we're searching for in a new relationship. From a practical point of view, our past histories (we're not twenty anymore) and the fact of gender discrepancy (there are far more single women than men) make traditional remarriage less likely. Rather, we will begin to see more romancing, dating, and coupling without marriage. There will be more and more older women hooking up with younger men. Informal (and formal) share-a-man relationships will be popping up—especially useful for escorts to social outings, dinners, concerts, and such. Same-sex relationships, mainly women with other women, will offer companionship for travel, education, and social events.

A minority will find the opportunity for remarriage. If one or both partners have lost a previous spouse to either divorce or death, we'll find significant issues that must be addressed. The major causes of failure in remarriages relate to feelings carried over from former marriages. Both partners in the new union must work to focus on each other's positive characteristics. Next come the pragmatic concerns. Both participants will have long histories of financial arrangements, family entanglements, and social circles. To merge these two worlds into one, in which all are happy and satisfied, is a daunting task. We must communicate with our new partners before the marriage and be very specific about each of these areas. Prenuptial agreements are recommended to give structure to these understandings.

If we approach the bonding process with all the wisdom we can muster from our lifelong learning, and we open ourselves to all the workable options, we'll increase our odds for a happy ending.

65 Consider a Pet

Pets can add unconditional love and unexpected delight to our lives. If we find ourselves in need of another relationship in our retirement, a pet may be an excellent choice. It could be a cat or dog, or a more exotic animal.

The trick to being satisfied with a pet is to choose an animal that suits our emotional needs and our lifestyles. For example, do we want one that is dependent or independent? Do we want one that can play? Do we want one that we can stroke? Do we want one that comes at our command? Do we want one that guards our house? Are there restrictions where we live, such as on size and noise? Are there leash laws? What options are available for the pet when we travel? For long-term satisfaction, it pays to research what types of animals best match our requirements and to make a rational choice instead of an emotional one.

If we make a good choice, pets can benefit us physically and emotionally. Researchers have discovered that stroking an animal can lower our blood pressure. Pets can bring us healthful smiles and make us laugh at their capers. Pets can make us feel more secure. They can be companions, offering a different form of friendship. Walking a pet can get us out of the house and help us make new acquaintances. Pets can even be substitutes for children.

Generally, a pet will never fail to meet our expectations. It listens to us, acting as if it understands what we're saying and empathizes with what we're feeling. It stays with us through good and bad times. Its dependability gives us a sense of emotional balance, strength, and stability.

In return for these powerful personal benefits, there are obligations in pet ownership. The care and feeding of animals vary. A lot of people underestimate the costs of food, grooming, and veterinary services. The physical and emotional needs of animals differ, too. Some animals need more space (living and roaming) than others. Some animals require the construction of structures such as pens and barns. Some animals can spend time by themselves while others pine for companionship. All these factors need to be considered and handled responsibly.

If we have the time and means, sharing our lives with a compatible pet may be one of our most rewarding experiences.

66 Connect with the Natural World

During retirement, rediscover that connecting with nature can be one of our most enriching activities. It can be as simple as observing the plants and animals around our homes: watching birds flit from branch to branch and listening to their calls, laughing at the friskiness of squirrels, witnessing a spider construct its web, noticing a plant pushing its way through the earth, savoring the display of spring and summer blossoms, reveling in a rainbow or fall colors, appreciating the stark beauty of winter, observing the changing light of sunrises, sunsets, storms, moonlight, and starlight.

Take a walk or hike to a particularly rewarding view of a waterfall or a gorge. Along the way, absorb the peacefulness of the forest, discover carpets of wildflowers, maybe catch a glimpse of a deer. Sometimes, such moments can surpass the sought-after vista. Other times, we bask in the destination, whether it's the top of a mountain or the edge of a canyon.

Trips to different locales can be eye-opening. How different the sandy beach and desert are compared to wooded mountains. In each ecosystem, find sets of plants and animals living in balance with one another. For example, in the Sonoran desert, there's a long-nosed bat that pollinates the flowers of the gigantic Saguaro cactus. We satisfy our curiosity. We get caught up in our sense of wonder. We find surprise, sometimes awe.

Gardening helps fulfill the very human urge to be in touch with the earth. Create terrariums; design and plant gardens for flowers or vegetables; train shrubs and trees into bonsai shapes. Gardening can be personally advantageous. It provides good physical exercise as well as visual and gastronomic rewards.

Choosing activities that reconnect us with the natural world helps us understand the diversity and almost infinite variety on Earth. It teaches us respect and reverence. It helps us grasp the commonalities found in life cycles. It allows us to feel we belong in our surroundings.

The benefits of connecting with nature are abundant. Physically and mentally, we relax. We escape the stress of our daily lives. We feel at peace with the world. Our blood pressure lowers. Our minds entertain new thoughts.

Make getting in touch with the natural world a priority. Enjoy all its beauties and benefits. It's the real thing.

PART SIX

Choose Enriching Activities

"I don't have the time or patience anymore to spend my limited hours on meaningless pursuits."

RETIREE, AGED SIXTY-SIX

67 Master What Brings Pleasure

Feeling fully alive and merely existing are opposites. What makes the difference between these two feelings is the filling of one's life with a range of pleasurable activities. Of course, what brings one person enjoyment can be different from what brings another individual satisfaction. Most contented people can agree, however, that treating oneself well is of paramount importance.

Here are some simple pleasures shared by many people:

- laugh more often
- laugh longer and louder
- prepare fresh foods in season
- take oneself out to dinner
- drink a glass of fine wine
- use good china, crystal, and linens on occasion
- buy oneself a gift (magazine, book, CD, home accessory, or clothing item)
- listen to music
- move with the music—dance!
- soak in a hot tub or bubble bath
- watch the sun rise and set
- sunbathe—maybe even in the nude
- watch birds or other animals in natural settings
- take a walk, hike, or trip

- reward oneself with a special day
- remember fun things from childhood

Each of us can expand this catalog of marvelous activities to please ourselves. List everything that feels good or fulfills a need. Fantasize the perfect life. To master what brings us pleasure at this stage in our lives, we may try things we've never tried before. Be open to those new experiences!

Learn to detach from our concerns and let the experiences fill the senses. It's called "letting go." Breathe deeply and float with the sensation. This perception can help turn one's pains into pleasures. Savor the solitude and magnitude of these moments.

Many activities provide opportunities to "lighten up." Learn to laugh and play more with other people. Seek to expand relationships with new acquaintances who enjoy the same activity or activities.

Other experiences allow us to explore our kinship with all life. We find commonalities with people, animals, and plants. We see our position in the matrix of life. We become more humble as we appreciate the earth, its environments, and its geological progressions.

While discovering which pleasurable activities are the most beneficial to us, we can rate each one on our list by how much it raises our self-esteem, emotional satisfaction, mental stimulation, creative expression, sense of fun and adventure, physical fitness, social interaction, and spirituality. The activities that increase our well-being will continue to bring us the most joy and satisfaction. Nourish oneself with these experiences. For the emptiness and harshness of life, our pleasures can be great antidotes.

68 Stretch the Pleasure Quotient

Rarely does anyone suggest that we increase the amount of pleasure we can tolerate. Yet, this ability to stretch one's acceptance of pleasure is a key secret to more fully enjoying our lives and our retirement. Most of us have become well acquainted with the work ethic founded on the "no pain, no gain" principle. There is validity to postponing immediate pleasure—if one can obtain greater satisfaction from the ultimate goal. However, engaging in unpleasing activities can often be a sign of masochism and poor mental health. Taking pleasure is a positive sign that reaffirms our belief in ourselves and in the beauty of life.

During retirement, we can shed our old limits and seek to go beyond them. We welcome excitement, risk rejection, challenge our habits, and seek authenticity. First, we give ourselves permission to enjoy. Next, we take a step. The step can be as simple as trying a new cuisine or having a sensual massage. It may involve travel or interacting with new people. It can require us to try a new creative task or to change our personal appearance. What it must include is the opening and widening of the avenues where we find pleasure.

Perhaps all this talk about pleasure sounds too hedonistic. Let's put it in perspective. Reflect on some of the more grating characters we've encountered in our lives. Think of those who were negative, ill-tempered, and ugly to others. Their one commonality is their unhappiness. Now consider the happy, fulfilled individual. He or she is one who seeks and welcomes pleasure. Once accustomed to this high level of pleasure, the person accepts it as the norm and attempts to create pleasure in most circumstances. Which do we desire as a goal for ourselves? As pleasure-filled people, we're better companions, relatives, and neighbors.

So, we measure our capacity for pleasure. How much time each day are we finding pleasure? How many ways are available for us to find satisfaction? Let's begin to add a few more minutes, perhaps one more enjoyable experience each week. We can bring ourselves to an even higher level of fulfillment.

69 Explore Hobbies and Recreational Activities

Retirement is the time to open up our world to new and exciting experiences. We can feel free to pursue our interests in several directions. We might rekindle our flame for a hobby that was ignored for too long. Picking it up again, we feel invigorated. We could tackle a new pursuit, perhaps one for which we once thought we had no talent. These fresh endeavors can provide both pleasure and healthy learning.

Our choices of hobbies and recreational activities can satisfy many personal cravings. Our physical bodies require exercise, so we make our choices accordingly. Think of the possibilities besides walking. We could hike or backpack, play tennis or golf, bicycle, swim, ride horses, ski, ice skate, or dance. There are games like Ping-Pong and horseshoes, sportsmen pursuits of fly-fishing and bow-and-arrow hunting, athletic possibilities like track and field and softball. Even traditional chores such as working around the house and gardening can provide physical exercise and emotional satisfaction.

Our pursuits might also include several that emphasize rest and relaxation. We could become collectors—of baskets, black-and-white photographs, stamps, or coins, to name a few possibilities. (The search is often more fun than the actual collection!) We can attend musical and theatrical productions or visit museums and galleries. We might enjoy nearby public lands (national/state/local parks, forests, wildlife refuges) while observing wildlife and photographing nature.

Other choices might develop our capabilities for self-expression. We can write—fiction or nonfiction, a book or a letter. We can play or compose music. We can act or give a dramatic reading. We can create art, take photos, or learn a craft such as wood carving, wood turning, pottery, weaving, or stained glass. We can cook, sew, or take gardening to a new level of beauty and function.

Our social lives can benefit from our choices. We could join interest groups (discussing books, films, investments, or various hobbies) or take aerobic classes at a gym or senior center. We could go to picnics and potluck dinners. We could get involved with a social or environmental cause. Our extended families and neighborhoods provide additional opportunities.

Hobbies will require us to keep learning. There are course offerings from local institutions or Elderhostel centers that combine the learning with the hobby. We can choose activities that demand a high level of thinking, such as chess, strategy gaming, computer programming, or specialized research. The public library and the Internet can be terrific resources in the process as well as give us new ideas.

When we follow a wide range of hobbies and recreational activities, we energize ourselves and elevate the satisfaction received from our retirement.

70 Do Something Wild

Children rarely have to be reminded to do something wild; usually, it's just the opposite. Adults, on the other hand, wrap themselves in a cloak of responsibility and may lose their sparks of spontaneity. When we reach retirement, it's another opportunity to indulge in a few unfettered, impulsive moments. We may discover an exhilaration for life not felt in many years.

Each of us has our own definition of what's wild and daring. To some, going to a late-night movie sounds pretty wild. For others, it might mean an impromptu trip to a remote island. We're searching for fascinating possibilities outside our normal range of day-to-day life.

Let's get in touch with our secret passions, which have often been hidden beneath our "proper" exteriors. For a person who's the model of neatness, a secret desire might be a long camping trip or volunteer project where showers and other conveniences are left far behind. For one who schedules every minute of the day, it might be a whimsical afternoon in the city. One retiree, who felt that she typified the reliable mother, planned and took a trip to Russia without ever hinting to her children that she was even remotely interested in traveling. She considered it a great thrill.

Think through all the possibilities. We're not trying to find a new hobby or avocation—simply fresh and exciting experiences. We're attempting to let go of old value judgments and look at the world anew. If we've been a bit prudish in our lives, we might try a nude beach or club. Retirees who've visited such places have found the high level of body acceptance a refreshing change from the dress-for-success world. If we've only experienced one type of religious activity, we could attend services from totally different cultures. We can go all out for a costume party, write a daring letter, prepare a creative meal, surprise an old friend, or get a massage. Think even wilder and consider going on a safari, skydiving, or training for the Senior Olympics.

When we engage in what we consider novel and outrageous behavior, we learn and grow. We also have fun.

71 Take Small Steps Toward New Endeavors

We've decided what we want to do in our retirement. We're going to climb Denali. We're going to try out the entire *Kama Sutra* on our mates. We're going to write a bestseller. We're going to open our own businesses. Before we embark on an ambitious endeavor, however, it may be helpful to break it into manageable steps.

First of all, we must do our homework. What equipment will we need? What preparations do we need to make? What are we likely to experience? We need to be realistic. Weigh the best-case scenario against the worst-case scenario. More than likely, the reality will fall somewhere between the two. It may be helpful to write down the possibilities.

Focus on the dream. Read articles and books. Talk to others whose experiences may help us along the way. Be sure to include others who may be affected by our plans.

If we find ourselves procrastinating, it may be because we fear the unknown. If so, we can do lots of little things to broaden our experiences. Begin with our daily lives. For example, we can alter our schedules, drive new routes, and shop different places. We can buy unusual foods and unconventional clothes. We can spend time with younger people. We can associate with different races or study other religious beliefs. Let's open ourselves up to new experiences. In the process, we shake ourselves out of our ruts and out of our fears, so we can get on with achieving our dreams.

The next step is to test the waters to make sure we really want to pursue a dream, particularly if the dream involves big changes to our lifestyle or big investments of money. For example, if it's full-time travel, we might take a monthlong trip to find out how it feels to be homeless—before selling the house. We rent or borrow any necessary equipment. If our dream is to go back to school and earn a doctorate, we could take a course or two and determine if we still like all the work involved. If we think we want to move to a different region, we can rent an apartment for a year and experience all the seasons.

Once the trial of a potential endeavor is complete, we evaluate the experience. What did we like? What did we not like? How can we lessen the undesirable and heighten the pleasurable? Will the end result be worth all the effort?

Take these small steps before making any giant leaps.

72 Keep Learning

A retired friend remarked, "I learn the most from people who continue to learn all their lives."

That's an interesting statement and an especially revealing one to us retirees. We do learn more from people who continue to engage life by assimilating and sharing as much as they can. These people may be generalists, expounding on a broad range of topics from food to travel, or specialists, focusing on a specific interest such as digital photography.

Why do these people seem to have more to offer than others? By learning new ideas and making firsthand observations, their brains have become more active. Recent research indicates that stimulated brain neurons will actually regrow! In addition, many creative ideas come from beginners, people who have a fresh way of looking at things.

The avid learner can become a more fascinating individual whose companionship is sought out by other people. As we share fresh ideas, facts, stories, and experiences, pay attention to our listeners. Are they asking questions that indicate interest, or are they switching the topic of conversation? Or, worse, are their eyes glazing over? We must realize, often, a little bit of information can go a long way.

How does one go about reawakening one's curiosity, one's thirst for knowledge? One way is to research a past area of interest. Our local libraries have many resources: books, magazines, newspapers, audiobooks, cassette tapes, music CDs, and videos. The results of this research may stimulate interest in other areas. Another method is to take intriguing classes at a community center, at a local college, or through a national or international program. Many institutions offer special courses or discounts to senior citizens. Two learning centers that involve new places, faces, and concepts are Earthwatch Expeditions and Elderhostel.

Another idea is to choose a hands-on activity such as wood carving, pottery, or blacksmithing. Take a course, or find a teacher who'll instruct one-on-one. Getting actively involved in such unfamiliar endeavors can stimulate other interests, too.

Seeking personal growth becomes a rewarding quest. Explore any interest. Read. Experiment. Analyze. Try again. Keep on learning. And, keep on sharing.

73 Contemplate, Read Books, Join Discussions—Expand Mentally

One of the greatest fears expressed by retirees is the loss of their mental faculties. Be it difficulty in remembering details or full-scale dementia, the prospect of encroaching senility can be terrifying. We can make choices now that will lessen the likelihood of such a bleak future. More and more research supports the notion that if we actively use our minds, especially with new topics and interests, we enhance our mental lives well into the future.

Let's not overlook the fundamental part of a healthy mental life—contemplation. Time spent in contemplation is our time to absorb, to grasp, and to reflect. We can sit by a stream, on a beach, in a desert, or on our decks or patios. Distractions fall away and we allow sensations, both internal and external, to wash over us. We can engage in contemplative activities such as going on a retreat, learning to meditate, or practicing yoga. This private time is when we think about our values, philosophies, and life's lessons. Perhaps we even plan for the future.

Many retirees use a second major tool to sharpen their mental acuity—reading. Try reading about a topic or in a genre that is totally new to us. We teach ourselves new skills, open ourselves to new cultures, rediscover various types of literature. Go to a library or bookstore and randomly pick a few volumes off the shelves. Peruse various reviews of books and pick ones that look interesting. On the Internet we find thousands of classic works that can be downloaded for free. Once we have reading material, we must allot the time to read. For some, reading is in lieu of television; others read only at bedtime. Some of us may wish to follow one retiree's advice: "I set aside a morning where I stay in bed and read—without guilt."

An active way to employ our minds and information we've learned is through discussion. We can even turn the mindless activity of watching television into something special by watching only movies or documentaries and talking about them with others. It becomes important to develop small groups that are comfortable discussing meaty topics. Often, libraries and bookstores feature book groups. There are special-interest groups and service clubs, too. The right mix of people can turn social events into something more meaningful. In addition, we can find discussion groups and chat rooms on the Internet. There, the communication is written, so it exercises another part of our brains.

Finally, it helps our minds when we organize and write down our thoughts. Keep the tools handy (paper, pencil, tape recorder, typewriter, and word processor) and use them. Follow Julia Cameron's advice in *The Artist's Way*. Set aside a block of time every morning to write without editing. Write about anything. Try to write three pages longhand. Over time, this process will unleash many new thoughts.

The retirees who appear most alert and most sharp, well into their later years, didn't get there by accident. They fed, massaged, and exercised their minds.

74 Learn How to Use a Computer

Retirement provides an excellent opportunity for neophytes ("newbies," in computer parlance) to begin using a computer as well as for seasoned users to learn new applications. Either way, computer mastery actively involves our minds in problem solving. We learn a new language and skills, develop lots of patience and persistence, and, with luck, turn out tangible products. Also, computer knowledge helps us keep abreast of current trends and provides one more link with the younger generation.

One of the first applications to learn is how the computer can help us communicate with others. The popularity of e-mail has skyrocketed, due to its quick informality. We dash off a note to anyone in the world and have it delivered instantly. The recipient chooses when to retrieve the note and when to reply. It's almost as quick as a phone call—and may be cheaper—but it doesn't intrude. Computers can also be used as word processors that help us produce letters, stories, even books. We can adorn our efforts with graphics and colors to the point of creating a professional layout. Our communication needs dictate how much we'll learn, but there's little that we can't do with today's software.

Another common use of the computer is to acquire and organize information. With Internet access, we have more information readily available than at any time in human history. The trick is to organize that information so we can turn it into knowledge. In the area of physical health, we can find the latest studies and the best research for almost any human ailment. Then there's legal data, investment ideas, tax tips, history, the arts, and more. If we desire to share information with others, we participate in chat rooms and newsgroups.

Many of us use computers for life's required tasks such as keeping personal financial records and preparing taxes. Personal financial software takes less time than a manual system, and it provides analysis and tools to enhance our financial well-being. A big bonus is that the tax chore is greatly lessened by appropriate tax software—often more accurate and thorough than the nonautomated alternatives. Other tasks, like making a will or living trust or creating a rental agreement or contract of sale, can be handled by personal legal software. Almost every aspect of daily living has a software program that can help.

As toys, computers can assist anyone who pursues a hobby or special passion. From genealogy to stamp collecting to photography to quilting, there is computer assistance to enhance one's interests. Of course, there's also the purely recreational pleasure of using a computer for individual or group games.

Computers do absorb chunks of our time. This time demand is especially apparent when learning something new or mastering a new program. Try to allocate the time necessary by eliminating a more mentally passive endeavor, such as watching television.

The cost of computers and access to the Internet has dropped dramatically over the years. The potential for mental gain has never been higher. Hop onto the information highway.

75 Record Life Experiences

With retirement comes many opportunities. One of these is to reflect on our lives to date, determine which of our talents and experiences might be of interest to others, and then share them in some loving way.

This could mean sorting through all the accumulated photographs, captioning them, and arranging them in an appealing fashion in a scrapbook. With a computer and color printer, some of these photos can be scanned and artfully manipulated (enlarged, reduced, sharpened, or filtered), then printed. The resulting images can be printed on quality papers for note cards, scrapbooks, or picture frames. They can even be printed on magnetic sheets for remarkable refrigerator magnets. Get innovative with ways to share the images with friends and family members. To perform these tasks, we need a scanner and image-editing software (often free with the scanner). Another idea is to produce a family slide show, using scanned photographs and a special computer software program.

The video camera presents many prospects. Write a script, reenacting a special event. Videotape old photos, then cleverly combine them with current footage of places, people, and pets to produce a lively and interesting show. Shoot other experiences worth sharing with the family, such as the younger generation wearing the older generation's clothes, and vice versa.

Audiocassettes are appreciated, too. Reminisce with or interview an elder, recording the session to share with others. Make the cassette come to life by enclosing a talked-about item with the tape—for example, an LP record, a hat, or a toy. Another possibility for sharing is to write a story and read it out loud for grandchildren and other youngsters. Similarly, compose and perform a musical piece.

Written accounts of our lives may be valuable to family and friends. Again, the computer has greatly simplified the process of writing, editing, proofing, and printing an autobiography. We can create stories, too.

The trick to making these sharings interesting to others is to come up with good ideas and creative ways to express them. Whatever we decide to share, we must be our own best critics.

76 Attend Social Gatherings and Cultural Activities

Going out is beneficial to our psyches and our bodies. Part of it is the change of environment. Another part is the stimulation our minds receive from interaction with other people and from appreciation of others' efforts. All combine to improve our attitudes and, consequently, our bodies.

Social gatherings can run the gamut from having a cup of coffee or a glass of wine with the person next door, to attending a party or organization meeting, to participating in a celebration such as a wedding or a holiday feast. These times together can be with family, friends, old acquaintances, and new ones. Often, the event allows us to make friends with individuals younger than ourselves, an important consideration as we age.

These social opportunities help us remain engaged with life outside of ourselves rather than isolated in our homes, where it's easy to turn inward and focus on our personal heartaches and physical pains. Attending social events can help us out of these funks. We learn firsthand what other people are feeling, thinking, and doing rather than hearing second- or thirdhand news from a radio or television.

Cultural opportunities can expose us to new experiences. Maybe we've never heard an opera or a modern jazz session. Perhaps we've never seen a modern dance performance or the works of an acclaimed artist. Possibly, we've never viewed the treasures of a past civilization. Such opportunities challenge our minds and senses.

As we retire and age, maintaining positive attitudes and optimal health becomes more important to our quality of life. We want to live zestfully. We want our bodies to function smoothly. We want to be pain-free.

Recently, the Harvard University School of Public Health released research on 2,800 elderly people over a thirteen-year time frame. The study concluded that even low-exertion social activity, such as playing bingo or cards, helped patients improve and prolong their lives.

So get out there and enjoy those activities. It's good for us!

77 Travel with Focus and Spirit

Travel brings us to the world in a way no brochure, book, magazine, newspaper, television program, movie, or Web site can. We experience a place firsthand—its environment, culture, foods, clothing, music, dances, and ceremonies. We can become caught up in this new location that's different from our hometown. The experience broadens us, making us more aware of human commonalities as well as differences.

In our retirement years we're less restricted by time, allowing us to travel more often—for longer periods and greater distances. Many retirees choose to travel full-time, selling their homes and purchasing recreational vehicles. These motor homes are best used where roads are in good condition and gasoline is reasonably priced. More retirees maintain their homes but take dream vacations or cruises. Some retirees opt for extended travels, driving, boating, or flying to exotic locations and living as if they were inhabitants of that area. Still others like to take courses through Elderhostel, perform volunteer work through Earthwatch, or join youth hostels.

However we choose to travel, it's desirable to have a purpose other than gawking at the natives. This focus might be recording folk songs or stories; studying great works of art; photographing events, people, animals, landscapes, or flowers; following in the footsteps of explorers; visiting religious sites; or achieving an experience like no other, such as hiking the Grand Canyon or running with the bulls at Pamplona. The focus provides new learning and meaningful ways to relate to other people, whether they're residents or fellow travelers.

Whatever our focus or destination, travel can be full of challenges. We're not in total control. We're in new locales without our tried-and-true routines. To enjoy the process, it's important to maintain an open mind, an even disposition, and a fun attitude. Such spirit will carry us over or through most obstacles, opening a world of adventure.

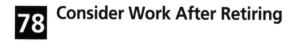

78 Consider Work After Retiring

Some of us find our work so rewarding, we want to continue well after the typical retirement age. If there's nothing else we'd rather be doing, this continuation will serve us well. We could also consider a new job, either full- or part-time. We may find that the structure of a job keeps us engaged in activities, involved in a social setting, and physically more active. One of our passions may develop into a new career. We might need additional income to make ends meet. Whatever the rationale, a number of us will be working for pay even during our "retirement" years.

To ensure we're making the right decision, we must assess ourselves. What are our best skills? How can those skills be used in business? What type of work provides the most satisfaction? What other kinds of activities do we want to do, and how much time will they take? Once we have a clear picture of our desires, we assess the job market.

Most jobs are filled through personal connections. If we're searching for a new opportunity, we network. We tell everyone we know that we're looking for a specific type of job. If we've relocated to a new area, we make an extra effort using groups such as the local chamber of commerce, professional associations, and service clubs. We carry a business card, print a well-written résumé, and are prepared for interviews at all times. We're ready to learn new skills to keep us on the cutting edge of technology.

Our avocations and favorite interests may lead us toward starting our own businesses. Entrepreneurial roles are laced with special rewards and numerous difficulties. A small business has little room for error. We must thoroughly understand our product or service and how it fits into the market. If our plan is so great, why isn't everyone already doing it? Also, we must deal with business decisions such as zoning, licensing, taxation, legalities, and accounting. We must ensure that we have adequate finances to carry us, as undercapitalization is the leading cause of failure for the small business. Still, we can flourish if we remember the secret of business success—give people more than they expect and do it cheerfully.

We must give ourselves permission to try new outlets to transform our lives. These outlets may involve engaging in for-pay work. The decision to work or not is best made rationally and unemotionally.

79 Volunteer

When we retire, we may be offered many opportunities to volunteer our time. This is good, unless we do not know ourselves well enough to say "no" to prospects that do not suit us. Of course, volunteering or performing unpaid work will benefit others. For us, it can be an opportunity to give back to our communities and contribute to society. In the process, we learn new skills and make new friends.

How else can volunteering help us? One study reported that 95 percent of participants who volunteered showed a decrease in chronic pain and an increase in optimism. Another study of 2,700 retired men over a ten-year period revealed that volunteers had a death rate two and a half times lower than nonvolunteers. In addition to these very physical benefits, volunteer work provides structure to our day and week. It also gives us a sense of purpose.

Volunteer opportunities abound: medical organizations (such as Red Cross, hospitals, nursing homes, mental health clinics); violence prevention organizations (Humane Society, National Coalition Against Domestic Violence, Parents Anonymous); environmental groups (Earthwatch, Audubon Society, Sierra Club, Greenpeace, Nature Conservancy); science museums; garden clubs; youth groups (Girl Scouts, Boy Scouts, Big Sisters, Big Brothers, Found a Friend); public schools and youth camps; museums of all types; volunteer programs in federal parks (National Park Service, National Forest Service,

Bureau of Land Management, Army Corps of Engineers); public service programs, which include the Service Corps of Retired Executives (SCORE), Active Corps of Executives (ACE), Peace Corps, Corporation for National Service (AmeriCorps), Volunteers in Service to America (VISTA), Retired and Senior Volunteers (RSVP), Foster Grandparents Program, and the Senior Companions Program; political groups (League of Women Voters, Democratic Party, Republican Party, various candidate campaigns); senior associations (AARP Volunteer Talent Bank, senior centers); and other local civic, political, religious, and charitable organizations.

Take responsibility and fill responsible posts. We can survey the field and choose about which something we feel good. To do this, we broadly evaluate our likes and dislikes, our abilities and limitations, as well as our motivations. Next, we categorize our likes into fields of activity such as agriculture, medicine, religion, art, music, or communications. We consider the organizations that make substantial efforts in our interest areas. Finally, we look at the specific jobs in terms of their compatibility with our talents and preferences as well as our schedules. Remember: the organization wants the match to be good, too.

If we find no organization that fits, we might start our own. When Maggie Kuhn was forced to retire from her job, she formed the Gray Panthers, who put a stop to mandatory retirement, among other accomplishments.

Most older people perform productive work. Productive work is any activity, paid or unpaid, that generates goods or services with economic value. According to the 1998 MacArthur Foundation study, 80 percent of retirees report more than 500 hours of productive work per year, and 40 percent report more than 1,500 hours per year.

Take this chance to make a difference in our lives and in the lives of others.

80 Follow a Passion

The time to follow our passions is now. Retirement is the place where we ditch all the old excuses like raising the kids, building a career, or keeping up with the Joneses. We reflect on what we feel passionate about and begin to take action.

A passion is our heart's desire, what we long to pursue. If we find we have nothing that we could classify as a passion, we can explore. We identify several interest areas that have intrigued us over the years, and we start investigating possibilities. We share our ideas with our partners and friends. Take several baby steps and contemplate the results. We will be able to find a direction.

Our passions can involve causes such as finding environmental solutions or strengthening the education of children. We could invoke new talents similar to those enjoyed by two retired doctors: one is exploring his lifelong passion with the world of literature; the other is adapting his fine motor skills into his passion for creativity by making furniture and sculpture. We could learn to play a musical instrument. We could learn a new language, perhaps sign language. We can dance, become athletes, or turn into outdoor enthusiasts.

Though we identify likely passions, we may still throw up roadblocks for ourselves, such as, "We lack the resources," "We'd travel if only we were rich," "We'd paint if only we'd had better training." We must realize that all of these obstacles are shams. We can travel close to home by camping; we can paint by picking up a brush and using instructional guides. One of the most curious aspects of following our passions is that the resources do seem to appear when they are required. Perhaps we need to take that leap of faith. After all, what have we got to lose?

When we follow our bliss (philosopher Joseph Campbell's word for passion), we'll find ourselves becoming more and more self-directed. The surrounding society may even appear out of step. What's happening is that instead of being tossed about like some rudderless ship, we're sailing on a clear course—what a wonderful gift to ourselves and those around us.

81 Get Involved in Meaningful Activity

When our lives feel vital and full of meaning, we enjoy a great retirement. One of the most common complaints of unsuccessful retirees is the feeling of uselessness. It's up to us to steer ourselves onto the great retirement track and away from this dead end. We must find activities that draw our support and energies. We need to have purposes beyond ourselves.

It's never too late to get involved. As one aged seventy-plus retiree shared, "If you continue to stay focused on yourself, you're guaranteed to be miserable."

One way we help ourselves is by helping others, one-on-one. We find people who need some type of assistance. Our involvement can be basic, like reading, coaching, or tutoring. It may involve visiting or providing transportation. It might be assisting with chores, giving financial advice, or furnishing other special expertise. We can help neighbors, family members, or strangers. They could be younger or older. Groups within social-services departments, churches, schools, and day-care centers provide us with many opportunities. Each of us has much to offer; we simply need to find the will and the time.

Our communities can also use our assistance. We find parks that need a cleanup, a class that needs to be taught, thrift stores that need staffing, committees and boards that need ideas and action, elected offices that need a new type of candidate. We discover we can make a difference.

There's a good chance we won't be able to change the world. We can, however, identify what we think are the most pressing societal problems and search for local solutions. If we hold environmental destruction as a major concern, we work locally to protect a stream, clean up a dump, or improve the recycling rate. If we believe family disintegration is harming children, we become active in a community center or youth organization. Whatever the large problem, there's a local action we can take. And by taking action, we help solve problems—and help ourselves in the process.

Find some causes and get involved. It's a surefire method to make our lives feel fuller and more meaningful.

82 Take Action

The nineteenth-century British politician Benjamin Disraeli said, "Action may not always bring happiness; but there is no happiness without action." All of our retirement plans and goals mean nothing until we begin their implementation. And, our situation changes when we commence a definitive course of action.

No matter what our age, there is still so much we can do. We take action by going to a new lookout to watch a sunset, picking up the phone to call an old friend, getting out of the house to visit a museum, or starting a new course of study. Big or small, making the move is the key.

When we find ourselves lagging on setting our plan in motion, we repeat our resolve again and again. Say it a hundred times a day until it generates the first tangible step. Affirming or asserting our goals does not guarantee our follow-through, but it often helps.

To avoid further procrastination, we focus on a single goal or project. If it's a complex project, we break it down into manageable steps. We start today. If the goal is to create a family album, we begin by assembling the first twenty photos found in our disorganized drawer of images. If the project is to learn a foreign language, we take a trip to the public library, check out a beginner's book, and read the first chapter. If we want to exercise, we fit in a long walk today. Whenever we act, we must avoid being too serious. It is permissible to pat ourselves on the back and enjoy the process.

By taking action, we also receive numerous chances to make mistakes. Over the years, however, we may have created an obsession for being correct. While we recognize that perfection is unobtainable, we continue to deny ourselves action for fear we may appear foolish or incompetent. At this stage of our lives, we can afford to take a few risks. Critique our bumblings with humor and we'll learn from our progress. We'll experience far more regret and guilt by not taking an opportunity than we ever will in making the attempt.

Let's remember that heroes are ordinary people who have taken action in spite of the consequences. Let's make our retirement more active, more fun, and more heroic.

83 Develop More Persistence

To get what we want in our retirement, whether it's consummating a lifelong dream, improving relationships, getting in shape, or learning something new, takes a lot of hard work. We can prepare ourselves for how mentally and physically demanding the process might be.

The first stage is a mental one, and it's a crucial one. We determine what we hope to achieve. Is our endeavor worthwhile? Is it one for which we have talent? Most tasks are 1 percent inspiration and 99 percent perspiration. Taking time to evaluate the merits of a project will keep us from pursuing unsuitable ones and allow us to put our time and effort into those that truly complement us.

Persistence means working at our ambition daily, being brave when meeting discouragements, continuing no matter what, determining the next step, figuring out how to overcome an obstacle, thinking creatively, and refusing to say, "I give up," "I can't," or "Yes, but . . . "

When we're feeling close to defeat, we gain inspiration from the collective wisdom of others. One sixty-four-year-old tells us, "Nothing of value comes without effort." Writer Kin Hubbard states, "There is no failure except in no longer trying. There is no defeat except from within, no really insurmountable barrier save our own inherent weakness of purpose." Find more motivation by reading articles and books, listening to audiotapes, watching videotapes, taking courses, finding a mentor, and talking with acquaintances.

Accept that our desired goal may take longer than we like. It's a fact that our physical reactions and mental processes may be marginally slower than when we were younger. Let go of these concerns. What we're after is the end result, and with persistence we can get there.

As humorist Josh Billings says, "Consider the postage stamp . . . it secures success through its ability to stick to one thing until it gets there." If we define our goals and practice persistence, chances are good that we, too, will find success.

84 Store Up Good Memories

Several adults were prodding young children to act like various animals for a forthcoming play. It wasn't going well. Was it worth the hassle? One of the wiser adults responded, "Of course it's worth it. We're building memories. When these kids are older, what are they going to remember—the usual day-to-day stuff or the time they were a giraffe in this play?" As adults, we can focus on building good memories, too. When we do, our retirement gains a new dimension.

Good memories stand out because of their specialness, unexpectedness, or novelty. Elaborate undertakings may disappoint; simple, stirring moments seldom do. Take advantage of opportunities such as watching a rare meteor shower or attending an uncommon musical performance. Simply changing our focus to the task of making something special can rejuvenate interest. Bring this positive attitude to regular occurrences such as family gatherings or holiday celebrations and look for chances to make them into good memories.

Retirement allows time for reflection on the past. When we choose to recall positive achievements and compliments, we find it satisfying. If we dwell on rejections and disappointments, we become crotchety or depressed. All lives are full of highs and lows. Take control of our selective memory process.

We can do more than store and recall good memories; we can document them. Photos, slides, videos, recordings, memorabilia collections, clippings, and other tangible artifacts could be organized as a memory project. We may find we want to create an exhibit like a scrapbook, quilt, or multimedia show. We can write our autobiographies. One retiree spent an hour a day typing his memoirs as an intellectual exercise (teaching himself how to type and use a computer, stretching his memory cells). He found that in recalling his past, he had to process the impact of each event on his life. The experience was very positive and therapeutic.

By creating and retrieving good memories, we are not seeking to dwell in the past but to fully appreciate our rich lives. Let's get out there and make something worth remembering.

PART SEVEN

Create Quality Living Space

"You know you've found a good place to live when you get an overwhelming sensation of 'This feels right.' And, most of my friends who've found their special place also report it's naturally beautiful."

RETIREE, AGED SEVENTY-NINE

85 Know What Makes a Good Home

During our retirement years, many of us will consider relocating our homes. To help make the result of our decision a happy one, we must ask ourselves, What makes a good home? If we don't have one now, why is that? By relocating, will we be running away from something or running toward something? We must know what we're looking for. And, we must be willing to make changes to accommodate our desires.

At different times in our lives, we look for different things. For example, at one point we want a new, even exotic, experience. At another time, we seek the comfort of familiarity. At a later date, we wish to rid ourselves of home maintenance demands. Still later, we need physical assistance.

Wherever we make our homes, they must feel comfortable. They must satisfy our physical, mental, and emotional needs. They must allow us to perform necessary, day-to-day tasks and still have time to do what we please. They must fit. We must not feel lost in them nor restricted by them. Our homes can integrate into our lives, not control them.

Options include single-family homes, condominiums, mobile homes, recreational vehicles, boats, apartments, and shared housing. Possibilities can be found in retirement communities or highrises. We can buy or we can rent. We could choose another place in the same town, move to a foreign country, or travel full-time. The spectrum is almost endless.

Realizing there is no perfect place, we analyze other important features to be at our happiest. Consider the agreeability of climate and geographic surroundings, recreational and cultural opportunities, part-time job and volunteer prospects, availability of necessary services, accessibility to transportation, proximity to family and old friends, safety concerns, and money matters such as cost of living and taxes. Gauge the warmth and aliveness of a potential community. Evaluate the possibilities for social and emotional support.

Being in touch with our preferences will help us make better decisions. Ultimately, though, it's choosing the place that feels best, a place where we can rest our bodies, hearts, and souls.

86 Surround Ourselves with Beauty

Since we only live once, we might as well make our lives the best they can be. One way to do this is to consciously surround ourselves with beauty, those qualities that please our senses.

There are many approaches to surrounding ourselves with beauty. For our homes, we select well-constructed spaces and fill them with functional items of good design. We add appealing artwork and thriving plants. For our communities, we choose places with pretty settings and predominantly good weather. For our dining pleasure, we buy the freshest foods and frequent the most highly rated restaurants. For cultural events, we assure ourselves access to musical, dramatic, and dance performances. For music at home, we pick the best recordings of favorite performers and works. For television viewing, we adopt habits that bring the best performances into our homes, such as watching special broadcasts and renting highly acclaimed movies. For reading pleasure, we purchase well-reviewed books or check them out from the library. For travel excursions, we drive or fly to locations touted for their natural attractions. The list of how to enhance the beauty in our lives goes on and on.

Surrounding ourselves with beauty is a philosophy of life that's doable thanks to the efforts of many people. Many manufacturers, service organizations, consumer groups, newspapers, and magazines make it their business to test and rate products and services, publishing the results for everyone's benefit. The trick to finding beauty instead of making do with less quality is to know what pleases us, to be aware of all our options, and to select the items that bring us the most satisfaction.

It's possible to turn beauty into a passion. One retiree purchased land that consisted of old, eroded cotton fields. Over thirty years (he's now aged ninety-three), he turned it into a nature preserve and sanctuary with towering trees, flowering bushes, ponds, and a gazebo. Then he established a foundation so that it would endure beyond his death. As he says, "Beauty comes in many forms. But for me, it's the plant form."

As the world population continues to grow, too often beautiful places are being altered by residential and commercial buildings. There are ways to surround ourselves with beauty in future years. We lobby our legislators for stronger efforts to protect and enhance our unspoiled landscapes. We financially support organizations such as nature conservancies which work to preserve the earth's natural attractions and healthy environments for the benefit of us and our descendants. We help clean up a waterway, beach, road, or vacant lot. Get involved in making the world a more beautiful place.

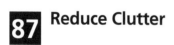 **Reduce Clutter**

To reduce clutter in our homes and in our lives, we must recognize it. It may be the newspaper that takes days to get recycled, the barrage of paper that arrives in our mailboxes, or the phone books that are strewn about. Clutter can be anything we've collected that serves little function in our lives. Or, clutter can be functional items that serve no aesthetic purpose.

Clutter is sometimes invited into our homes; for example, subscriptions to newspapers and magazines. One alternative is to have periodicals delivered to our local library. Another option is to read articles on-line in an electronic format.

Although it's often hard to control what comes into our mailboxes, we do have options about what we do with unwanted materials. If we look forward to controlling our mail, we'll find processing it a satisfactory experience. Most junk-mail items need not be opened. They can be thrown away. Try it. It feels good to not clutter our minds with offers for things we really don't need or want.

Sometimes, stuff we save for a good purpose can get out of control. It can be the coupons we're clipping for groceries and toiletries, the articles we're saving for our next project, or the materials we use to ship packages. In areas such as these, it's best to devote specific spaces to each purpose. For example, coupons can be organized in a handy file that can be carried into the store. Similarly, establish file folders for ideas on vacations, home improvements, garden plantings, craft projects, recipes, and so on. A file cabinet will keep this information at our fingertips—so much easier to find than if the clippings were stacked on top of one another on a table or shelf. When stuff such as packing material outgrows its allotted space, reorganize, recycle, or discard the excess. Often, small businesses that ship products will welcome extra boxes. Attempt to keep several sizes of boxes on hand and a small amount of bubble wrap or Styrofoam peanuts.

Items such as phone books or operating instructions need to be handy to the appliance. Try to locate these materials in the closest drawer or cabinet; rooms look better if such clutter is out of sight.

Look at drawers, cabinets, and closets with an analytical eye. It can be an enlightening experience to ask, "Why is this here?" "Am I using this?" "Do I need to keep this any longer?" "How much is enough?" It's amazing how much stuff can go.

Another tactic to prevent clutter is to not buy it. When shopping, ask, "Do I really need this item?" Whether it's a necessity or a nicety, know if the item is an addition or a replacement.

The trick with clutter is to recognize and control it—not let it control us. As with most material things, the more clutter we have, the less freedom we enjoy.

88 Consider All Housing Options

The most obvious housing option for retirees (and the most popular) is to stay put. Wherever we live and whatever we live in, we don't change a thing. The complete opposite of this status quo approach is to sell it all and take off for full-time travel, either domestically or worldwide. Between these two divergent options, we find a wealth of possibilities.

Many retirees seek a change in location—if not immediately upon retirement, then a few years down the road. We may seek less maintenance, a change in climate, a community with more offerings, or a better support system. We'll find many choices available. The three major options most will consider are a retirement area, a resortlike community, or a retirement center (sometimes called a continuing care retirement center).

Retirement areas are springing up throughout the world as local leaders find retirees to be a nonpolluting, renewable growth industry. As a result, many communities are beginning to offer services and housing alternatives that seniors will need and appreciate. Developers are producing retirement versions of traditional resorts. The most well known are the "Sun Cities," which are located in various southern states. Though appealing in their wealth of recreational and social offerings, they are usually age segregated, meaning retirees must make an extra effort to maintain contact with the younger generations. Those who desire a more complete support system, including assistance when health begins to fail, might consider a retirement center. Though expensive, the centers try to provide services geared to changing physical and mental needs.

Though these retirement areas may be appealing, let's not overlook other practical options. For instance, we could simply move within our local areas, choosing a place more suitable to our current needs, while continuing to benefit from our old circle of family and friends as well as our shopping and recreational favorites.

If we do relocate, we benefit from the wide range of housing alternatives. Camping or renting is a low-cost, temporary method of checking out a place before making a more permanent move. Our choices of domiciles are many: apartment, condominium, shared housing (living with others), cooperative (private quarters plus common areas), house (single family or multiple), recreational vehicle, mobile home, or boat.

Having a great housing experience during retirement requires thinking through all these options and reflecting on how well they fit our desires for our retirement lifestyle.

89 Relocate Realistically

The vast majority of retirees do not relocate. Those who do often move within the same community—to a smaller house or to a facility with services. There is, however, the lure of discovering a new place, creating a fresh start, and relaxing in paradise. With a little luck and some research, we find wonderful places to live.

As with all secrets to a great retirement, the fundamental key is knowing what we need and what we enjoy. Whether we're considering a Sun Belt condo on a boat canal, sharing space with family or friends, or moving to another country, we start with what's important to our happiness on a day-to-day basis. We could spend hundreds of thousands of dollars on a relocation only to find that the community's restrictions stop some of our favorite activities. Or, we might find the social or cultural opportunities to be less than we'd hoped for. We need to honestly reflect on what's wrong with our current locations and what we expect to be different in our new alternatives.

The best way to evaluate a potential move is through testing the waters. Rent for a period of time—several weeks or several seasons. Listen to people's experiences who've moved there previously. Use a "best places" list. The more we know, the more likely we are to make a good choice.

It's also helpful to look into future considerations in this new location. If we intend to stay there for more than a few years, we must keep in mind our changing needs as we age. Someday, we may require help with maintenance, housework, health, transportation, and other challenges that are not issues for us at the moment.

A realistic relocation includes understanding that our lifelong tendencies probably will not change in this new locale. If we're good with social interactions but also value moments of privacy, we'll want to choose with those preferences in mind.

We'll find that in most new situations, we'll literally be starting over. To fit in, we must earn the respect of others, not feel that we deserve it based on our pasts. Forget telling everyone "how it was done" where we used to live. The most successful technique for acceptance is giving. When we volunteer our efforts to help others unconditionally, even the most jaded old-timer will eventually acknowledge our presence.

With a pragmatic understanding of ourselves and our possible new communities, we can make an excellent relocation. And, let's not forget, it's not all or nothing. If it doesn't work out, we can move again.

PART EIGHT

Boost Potential

"As the saying goes, 'Old age is not for sissies.' I sometimes have to work harder to accomplish my goals, but then again, I've learned a bunch of tricks along the way."

RETIREE, AGED EIGHTY-SIX

90 Have Great Expectations

If asked, all of us would say we want retirement to be the greatest and happiest time of our lives. But have we expressed that expectation? Have we felt sufficiently confident in ourselves and in others to expect these years to be our best ones? Or have we allowed stereotypes of old age or accounts from others and the media to fill us with fear, causing us to expect less than the best?

From our experiences, we create personal beliefs that support what we think is best for us, family members, friends, neighbors, and others. If we want to see a change in our behavior or in that of others, we often have to start with ourselves, creating an impetus that ripples outward. We have to raise our expectations and let them be known.

One classic experiment in educational psychology gave teachers test scores for their new students. These scores were touted as accurate predictors of academic success. By the end of the term, there was a high correlation between the scores and the students' performances. Then, it was revealed that the "scores" were actually the students' locker numbers! Both teachers and students had performed to these random expectations.

Do not shortchange our retirement by having low expectations. To expect the best, we have to lighten up, be joyful, think positively, and express optimism and hope. One retiree declares, "I've learned that if I look for the worst in people, I'll find it. But if I look for the best, I'll find that instead." This retiree has learned that to a great degree, she can control the quality of what she experiences simply by expecting the best in others.

This retiree goes on to share, "When bad things happen, and they do, I try to learn the lessons but forget the experiences. That's easy to say, but hard to do. Sometimes, I must admit that I could have performed better in a situation. Then, I resolve to do better, raise my expectations of my behavior, then give it my personal best."

Let's keep our expectations high. We do reap what we sow.

91 Convert Negatives into Positives

As we grow older, we find ourselves saying "no" to opportunities we would have said "yes" to when we had boundless energy. We have to be careful to not allow saying "no" to become a habit, because disengaging ourselves from life brings unhappiness.

We were not born unhappy. If we've become unhappy, it's something we have learned over our lifetimes. Often, we're blaming others or situations instead of taking responsibility to learn from life. We're accepting passive roles instead of active ones; we're opting to rage against our pasts rather than live in the present and nurture our passions for the future. Though we may see the possibilities, we feel helpless to take action.

Knowing that discontent leads to depression, we must evaluate each prospect. Is it something we can do? Will it bring new possibilities and pleasures into our lives? Does it bring us closer to our goals and dreams? In the process of saying "yes" to more opportunities, we become more active, more passionate, more powerful, and more content individuals.

It's an interesting phenomenon: the way we choose to view the world *becomes* our world. If we look for the best in each and every situation, we find it. When we experience something we'd rather not or we catch ourselves expressing a negative thought, we can look at our fingers and list ten positive thoughts. In the process of looking for what's good, we become better instead of bitter.

Sometimes it's simply taking a moment to look more positively at an individual. For example, do we think of the person as hardheaded, or persistent? Nosy, or concerned? Odd, or creative? Is he or she more likely to change a troublesome behavior if we point out shortcomings or if we compliment strengths? Although we cannot make decisions for that person, we choose our own attitudes and behavior.

As a retiree shares, "I try to never underestimate the power of the human mind. I think that optimists live better and longer than pessimists. That's why I remain an optimist. My behavior may seem Pollyannaish to others. But, I believe my attitude has brought me many wonderful life experiences. I would suggest that others try it. They have everything to gain and nothing to lose."

Opportunities for happiness happen every day. We can convert negatives into positives. In our retirement, we can learn to see and do our best.

92 Confront Old-Age Stereotypes

There are numerous stereotypes, myths, or illusions about old age. Let's find out why some of these ideas are incorrect.

Illusion: Old Age Happens at Sixty-Five. Age sixty-five is a pivotal number as far as many governments are concerned. That's when people may start drawing governmental financial assistance and, possibly, medical assistance. Most of these social programs were set up in the first half of the twentieth century. Since then, because of medical advancements, people have enjoyed increased longevity and decreased illnesses. When we reach age sixty-five, we can either fall victim to the outdated notion that we're now old or embrace the current reality that we can have highly active lives well beyond the age of sixty-five. By example and action, we can fight discrimination against older people.

Illusion: Most Old People Are Decrepit. Knowledge about the crucial importance of exercise and diet is allowing people to maintain high levels of functioning as they age. While people may develop chronic health problems as they age, most are not limited by them. As a general rule, it is not until the last six months of life, as the body shuts down, that one experiences ailing health. In the meantime, it appears that if we expect more of our bodies, we obtain more.

Illusion: Most Old People Are Sexless. All recent studies show that older adults continue to enjoy sex—a lot. What is in the process of changing is society's perspective on sexual relationships among older adults. There is growing acceptance of unmarried or widowed people having sexual relations and, consequently, alternative living arrangements besides monogamous marriages.

Illusion: Most Old People Become Senile. The use-it-or-lose-it concept popularized by sex researchers holds true in other physical activities and in mental capacities. The benefit of aging is that we can apply our vast experiences to problems, more than compensating for any loss in learning speed. Research indicates it is important to continue learning new areas of knowledge. The more we work our brains, the more they will continue to work for us.

Illusion: Most Old People Are Boring and Monotonous. When we're around older people, we can inventory their "assets." We'll find an incredible array of physically able and mentally active people, with strong individual styles and preferences. We'll discover that each person is unique—not all alike or boring.

Illusion: Most Old People Are Unproductive. Retirees accomplish a lot of work—for personal and other-directed benefits. Current studies show that older workers produce as much (and often more reliably) than their younger counterparts. In the future, there will be a redefining of the word *productive*. Meanwhile, stay engaged in meaningful activities.

Illusion: Most Old People Live Close to Poverty. Generally, as most older people have more experiences to draw upon, so do they have more accumulation. Statistics show that from the poorest to richest classifications, older people have the most net worth. In the poorer classifications, it is appropriate to offer assistance.

For more information on recognizing and fighting old-age stereotypes, see books such as Mary Helen and Shuford Smith's *The Retirement Sourcebook*, John Rowe and Robert Kahn's *Successful Aging*, and Ken Dychtwald and Joe Fowler's *Age Wave*.

93 Heighten Curiosity

Curious people never seem to age mentally. They appear alive and alert to those around them. They rarely, if ever, get bored. Curiosity seems to be a trait all of us would want to strengthen.

When we exhibit curiosity, we demonstrate a desire to learn something. As children, we were curious about everything— how it worked, why it looked the way it did, what it could do for us. As we age, the curiosity may have become more restricted, focusing only on items close to our daily lives. With retirement, we can open up again to a whole universe of marvelous things to learn.

We start our curiosity sessions with personal favorites or familiar topics. We fill in gaps that have developed in some of our memories. Once we begin, our curiosity explodes. Reexamine that family tree and look for hidden stories, study what was happening during critical points of our lives, finish or retake a course of study that gave us fits many years ago.

One of the strongest ways to enhance our curiosity is to expose ourselves to new people and places. These experiences can occur near our own communities or in a foreign country. We seek more than passive observation; we want to research and explore. These people have faced similar problems and challenges, but they may have developed different solutions. We can "try on" their answers to more fully understand their lives. We could learn their language or dialect; enjoy a new cuisine; or study their architecture, agriculture, music, or religion. When we actively follow our curiosity, we rejuvenate our lives.

With libraries and the information resources of the Internet, we can stimulate our curiosity at will. Pick a few books at random or visit several unrelated sites on the Web. Chances are, there'll be topics that pique our interest. When looking up a word in the dictionary, roam the page and discover other words that are fascinating. Simply asking, "Why?" about a common occurrence can lead to intriguing research.

As Albert Einstein said, "The important thing is not to stop questioning. Curiosity has its own reason for existing. One cannot help but be in awe when he contemplates the mysteries of eternity, of life, of the marvelous structure of reality. It is enough if one tries merely to comprehend a little of this mystery every day."

94 Live in the Moment

Most of our lives, we've practiced the delay of gratification. What are we going to do when we grow up? Where are we going to school? How do we strengthen our career paths? Where are our kids going to school? Where will we retire? It's quite easy to let these forward-looking concerns dominate our lives to the point that we ignore the present. During retirement, the present becomes vitally important. As the American legislator John Randolph said, "Time is at once the most valuable and the most perishable of all our possessions."

While neither ignoring the past nor failing to plan for the future, we want to grasp that our life is *today*. If there is a tomorrow, it's a gift. We want to appreciate what one retiree observed: "People get in such a hurry to find the 'good life' that they often rush right past it." Or, as another put it, "The trip is often more fun than the destination."

To live in the present means to focus and become aware. We stop worrying about past or future events. If we come upon an accident or emergency such as a heart attack, we assist best when we concentrate completely on what's happening at the moment. We don't fret or panic, we stay in the present. When we converse with our families, we communicate effectively when we keep our attention squarely on the present interchange rather than delve back into old disturbing issues. If we are talking with members of the younger generation, we relate to their current ideas rather than constantly repeat what we used to do.

When we live for the moment, it becomes difficult to be unhappy. Our goal might be to totally enjoy each day rather than waiting for a special event. We don't have to postpone our happiness until the kids' or grandkids' next visit. We can celebrate our partners, our friends, and our families all the time—not just at anniversaries, holidays, or reunions. It sounds so simple: live in the present. Once we make up our minds to do it, it's easy.

95 Make Time an Ally

One of the most common perceptions of the nonretired population is that retired people have all the time in the world. Yet, many retirees tell us, "I've never been so busy." Is retirement a season of empty hours or a plethora of active moments? The successful retirees appear to be those who meet the time dilemma head-on and make it work for them so they are neither bored nor frazzled.

The first notion of time we must accept and practice in our lives is that it's never too late. We may have procrastinated in the past, but we can begin to take action today. Want to write poetry? Jot down a rhyme. Desire to lose weight? Change an eating habit over the next couple of meals. Thinking about a computer? Spend some time at a public library with a terminal. Have an unresolved conflict with family or friends? Pick up the phone or pen now. Retirement offers us that special gift, a second chance.

Another aspect of time to understand, as one retiree puts it, is to "learn how to hurry slowly." Savoring the moments, slowing down, and spending half our hours in quiet and calm—all depict a person who is living wisely. Some people are able to discover this reflective pace by adjusting daily schedules. Others need to allocate special days for these peaceful pleasures.

When we find things we really want to do, we'll find the time to do them. This is one of life's difficult lessons: no matter what people claim their dreams might be, their real dreams and values are expressed by how they spend their time. We may not be able to instantly achieve a dream, but if we're serious, we can take the first steps. If we truly desire to travel, we'll make an excursion, even if it's to a nearby park rather than around the world. If we have a passionate desire to read, we'll do it even if it requires reserving a small block of time in our daily schedules.

One retiree reviewed her appointment calendar for the previous year and made a list of the things she had done. In one column, she wrote down all of her less-than-wonderful experiences; in the other column, she listed the rewarding events. She was shocked at how much time she had squandered on the trivial and how little she had spent on her passions. This exercise gave her a new direction for the rest of her retirement.

Our retirement blossoms when we carefully nurture how we use our time. All of us have the same twenty-four hours each day to fill with activities of our own choosing. When we balance our reflective moments with our active ones, when our stated priorities coincide with our use of time, we find that time becomes our trusted friend.

96 Stay Engaged with Life

For many of us, retirement introduces an upheaval in our daily lives. Much of our world revolved around the job. Many demands were put upon us, and if we met them, we felt successful. Without this structure, we are faced with the challenge of finding new activities that allow us to remain engaged and feel productive.

To stay engaged means we raise our chances for successful aging. Many research studies have alluded to this relationship. The recent MacArthur Foundation Study on Successful Aging went further by concluding that attitude, diet, exercise, and engagement with the world around us will be the main contributors to the quality of our lives. The underlying construct is that all the engaged retirees are "doers." Interestingly, these "doers" are also the same people others find engrossing.

So, what can we do? How can we feel useful and engaged? How do we continue to participate in life? Some of us will focus on volunteer work or special activities that provide us the opportunity to give back. Others will seek for-pay work of some type—a variation of our former work, consulting, a new career—either full-time or part-time. A few may start up a new business. A handful will embark on a course of study. Many will pursue hobbies and pleasurable moments, weaving them into an active life. Some will travel extensively. We can choose any or all of the above to meld into satisfying experiences.

The broader our social contacts, the easier it will be to find opportunities. We can assist family and friends, mentor or tutor younger people, and find situations where we encounter strangers of all types. The more diverse our interactions, the more likely we'll stay involved with life.

As we age, we may find impediments to staying engaged. Unfortunately, throughout society, there rings the phrase "You're too old." The emphasis on youth and the stereotypes of aging serve to disengage people over age sixty-five from the mainstream. As the facts mount to refute these beliefs, this negative pressure will decrease in the years ahead. We can all heed the advice of one retiree who suggests, "Just think of yourself as self-employed. Your business is learning how to live a full life. Then, go from there."

Regularly, we'll need to monitor our level of involvement in our interest areas. It's all too easy to slip into a withdrawal mode and passively let our lives slip by. Let's stay engaged.

97 Practice Resiliency

Resiliency is the capability to recover quickly from misfortune. As we mature, we accumulate more unpleasantness, illness, and loss in our lives. The ability to bounce back to our usual, well-balanced selves becomes more and more important. From the earliest studies of long-lived people, resiliency has been mentioned as one of the prime characteristics.

To practice resiliency, we need to know ourselves pretty well. We must recognize when an event has affected us. Then, we must take steps to recover our normal natures. Compiled from various sources, here are some ways to enhance resiliency:

- remain realistic about life
- accept that catastrophes do happen
- realize that attitude is more important than luck or genes for personal health

- exercise patience
- maintain hope
- resist becoming anxious about events beyond our control
- practice relaxation techniques
- continue taking care of self (eating, exercising, and sleeping well)
- sustain interest in ongoing events
- encourage contact with family and friends
- avoid living in the past
- refuse to obsess
- keep producing our best
- when frustrated, focus on what we can do instead of what we cannot do
- create new routines, if needed
- avoid apathetic and hateful behavior in oneself and others
- learn to forgive
- give to others
- find strength in spirituality
- remember that, in time, the situation may become funny
- live one day at a time
- develop more joie de vivre
- laugh!

The rewards for practicing resiliency include improved mental and physical health and, consequently, longer life.

98 Know We Can Change at Any Age

That we retire from work does not mean we retire from life. We've been changing all our lives. We will continue to develop for the rest of our lives—unless we decide to stop growing. The clues to someone who has congealed are such phrases as "I'm too old,"

"If only I had started earlier," "I've always done it this way." Let's not fall into the trap of defeating ourselves before we even start.

Retirement brings different daily routines. It may be the perfect time to initiate additional, more personal modifications in our lives. We may want more moments of sanity and solitude. We may want more activity. We may want a more loving, more physically and emotionally satisfying emphasis in our relationships. We may want to go so far as to develop a new identity with different interests. Any of this is doable at any age.

Realizing that we continue to change, we accept our pasts as just that. It's past; it's over. Any past moment is no more important or powerful than the present instant or a future one. Although our pasts have a bearing on our lives, they do not control our lives. It's our beliefs, goals, and commitments that control our actions and, consequently, our lives. If we believe we can achieve a specific goal and we make a commitment to do so, we can change. We can do it right now.

It's important to not postpone making positive changes. It's important to not erect additional hurdles we'd have to cross over before accomplishing desirable changes. For example, try not to make change conditional on external events such as winning someone's approval or the lottery. Realize that one change can make another easier. And, there's nothing holding us back but ourselves.

Seize opportunities daily. Focus on the goal and all its possibilities. Think positively. Take action. Continue to look forward, not backward. Enjoy the process!

99 Realize Opportunities to Be by Oneself

While we were building a career, adjusting to marriage, or raising children, we fantasized about having time to ourselves. Now that we're retiring and facing not only hours but days to fill in some meaningful way, we're not sure we really want it—ah, the human conundrum! But wait, was life better when there were so many demands from family and work that they filled almost every minute? It helps to do a reality check every once in a while so we can savor what we've got.

What's different now is that we're in charge of structuring our lives and deciding how we spend our time. No longer are our families and jobs providing that framework. It's up to each of us to realize and act on the opportunities of being on our own.

We may or may not have a significant other to encourage us through this transition. If we are alone, it does not mean we have to feel lonely. Loneliness is a mental condition rather than an actual circumstance. We must remain open to possibilities for intimacy and friendship. In addition, we must develop the healthy practice of enjoying things by ourselves.

It's natural to feel some resistance at this change in our lives. In our discomfort, we'll go check on what others in the house are doing. We'll call friends to hear what they're accomplishing. We may stop by the old workplace to see what's going on there. It takes time to get over the messages of "I should be doing this" or "I should be doing that."

Eventually, we settle down and into a frame of mind where we're comfortable with ourselves. We begin to adopt daily and weekly routines that nourish us. We watch the sunset, soak in the bathtub, and prepare a favorite meal, perhaps serving it with linens and candles. We read, write in our journals, and look for spiritual opportunities. We find a place of sanctuary. We develop our sensory perceptions, enjoying the sound, smell, taste, look, and feel of things around us. We get in touch with our inner voices. We become stronger, mentally and physically. In the process of all this, we become good company for ourselves. Ultimately, we welcome these times of solitude.

100 Become Wise

One of the great positives about aging is that it provides us the opportunity to grow wise. Wisdom will not come automatically or easily, but it is within our grasp if we desire it.

The heart of wisdom is perspective. It implies we know what is important and what's trivial. We see a larger picture and grasp how a situation fits within it. Limitations and possibilities become obvious. Notice that wisdom does not require great intellectual power but rather a sense of balance. Both experience and knowledge may help, but they are not synonymous with being wise. As the philosopher William James said, "The art of being wise is the art of knowing what to overlook."

As we approach the challenge of becoming wise, we remind ourselves of the pitfalls of giving advice, especially to those younger than us. Unsolicited suggestions and unwanted comments on problems similar to those we've encountered do not constitute wisdom. As one retiree shares, "If you're going to give advice, be brief." We must know when to speak and when to listen.

If we want to make a wise decision, we first think broadly about all the available options. Second, we gather any essential information not already on hand. Third, we consider the long-term consequences of various courses of action. Fourth, we realize that any course of action must occur in the real world. Finally, we accept that all possible solutions will have strengths and weaknesses.

For example, how do we make a wise choice about what to do with a barren piece of land other than plant grass? Step one has us gather information about our favorite types of garden and natural areas—aquatic, annual, perennial, vegetable, exotic, and indigenous. We reflect on our desire to work outside, both now and in the future. Step two finds us researching the requirements (such as for soil, moisture, light, and maintenance) imposed by each type of planting in our climates. Step three has us look beyond the near term and calculate what will be the rewards versus the effort and cost over the years. Step four has us consider the likelihood of pests and diseases, and search for the correct combination of plant species, knowing we'll have to modify our plans as we learn. We accept there will be no perfect landscape, but we make wiser choices than if we had simply gone with our first notion.

Over the long term, we focus on what's important in our world and what isn't. When we maintain this perspective and use all of our experience, knowledge, and common sense, we will grow wise.

101 Make Life the Best

Remember all those admonitions from childhood? "Just do your best"; "Give it your best shot"; "Is this your best effort?" How many of us have felt guilt from the notion that we might not be living up to our potential? As we move into retirement, it may be time to revisit those homilies—without the guilt. None of us want to settle for an average retirement. We want one that's great. And that means we must give it our best. As one retiree pointed out, "Retirees can choose to be a park ranger or to be depressed, to write their memoirs or to be an alcoholic. There is no one around to choose for them, unless their spouses, children, or doddering parents want to take on the job."

It's all too easy to see where others have not given their best. Look at polluting plants, strip malls, sloppy construction, banal TV shows, sleazy tabloids, and on and on. All of us can create a list of pet peeves related to low quality and insensitivity toward the future. The common threads are a lack of vision, a focus on the short term, and a shortage of commitment to doing one's best.

A more difficult challenge is to turn away from the outside world and honestly hold up the same mirror to our own lives. All of our actions and decisions paint a portrait of ourselves. Is it the best picture we can imagine? Are we being authentic? Do we communicate our true feelings, go that extra mile, and take time to polish our actions? Can we spot our weak points where sloppiness in word or deed prohibits us from reaching our best?

In retirement, we can take the time to improve. Think of our possible refinements—a bit of extra effort in preparing a meal, a few moments helping someone, more time spent in laughter, more opportunities to show kindness and appreciation, or an attempt to listen better. Doing our best requires us to raise our standards and expectations. It's easy to become lazy, both mentally and physically, and take a path of convenience. When making decisions—be they common shopping selections, family interactions, election alternatives, investment decisions, or dream pursuits—we can apply the extra mental effort necessary to make a truly informed choice.

While the perfect retirement may be unobtainable, we can aim for it and, through perseverance, come much closer than if we had given up without any effort.

Afterword

If you practice these 101 secrets, you will be assured of a great retirement. Remember that you need to implement them, not just read them.

In our retirement, we've been living our dreams—traveling full-time across North America, keeping a journal, photographing the highlights and, now, sharing our experiences through words and images.

It's our hope that you, too, will achieve your dreams during retirement. If our book has helped you in a specific way or there are additional secrets you'd like to share, we'd love to hear from you.

Write or e-mail us:

Mary Helen & Shuford Smith
253 Judge Road
Tryon, NC 28782
maraford@alltel.net

AARP, study done on older Americans and sex, 93

accidental falls, caused by improper medications, 65

acquisition of material things, not overdoing, it, 36–38

action, taking, 131–132
    avoiding procrastination, 131–132
        knowing mistakes will be made, 132

active, staying, 57–58
    finding motivation for, 57
    getting out, 57
    stimulating mind, 58
    taking breaks when sitting for long periods, 57–58
    ways to increase activity level, 57

activist, becoming
    example of one retiree, 18–19
    as a meaningful activity, 131

activities
    contemplative, 119–120
    fulfilling, finding, 18
    hands-on, 119
    meaningful, getting involved in, 130–131
    recreational, 114–115
    seeking out pleasurable, 111–113

adding years to our lives, over the past century, 53

advertising
    common techniques used in, 78
    as form of brainwashing, 77–78

advice, pitfalls of giving unwanted, 160

aerobic exercise. *See also* exercise
    benefits of regular, 54, 59

age 65
    odds for women to live to 85 once they reach, 15
    stereotype regarding, 149–150

Age Wave (Dychtwald), 151

aging process
    accepting realities of, 81
    adjusting to, 9–10
    challenges of growing older, 7
    consumer products to help with, 6
    embracing as natural, 6–7
    emotional health, and, 50
    eyesight, changes in, 6, 9, 49
    face, changes in, 6–7
    harder to accept growing older, 49

    hearing loss and, 7, 9
    maintaining positive attitude about, 7, 49
    mental deterioration and, 51
    physical changes, 49
    physical skills lesson, 9–10
    sense of smell, changes in, 7
    sense of taste, changes in, 7
    short-term memory loss, 7
    surgical procedures to look younger, 49

airlines, offering senior citizen discount, 33

alarm clocks, using extra loud, 6

alcohol consumption, drinking in moderate amounts, 60

alive, feeling fully
    difference between merely existing and, 111

allergies, taking a hard look at pollen and mold, 60

American Association of Retired Persons. *See* AARP

American Diabetes Association, on avoiding sugars, 54

American Dietetic Association, on lowering fat intake, 54

American Red Cross, sponsor for CPR training, 61

anxiety, over having enough money to retire, 23–24

appreciation, showing, 75–76

arthritis pain
    be aware of hoaxes, 64–65
    strength training to help relieve, 54

Artists' Way, The (Cameron), 120

aspirin
    giving in emergency situation to heart attack victim, 61–62
    taking daily to reduce risk of heart attack, 54

assets
    having a detailed inventory of, 42
    keeping control over, 44

Attitude Factor, The (Blakeslee), 71

audiobooks
    listening to, 8
    making one of life experiences, 123

authors of this book,
    contact information, 163

automobiles. *See* cars

back exercises, doing may alleviate need
for surgery, 64
balance in life
becoming less judgmental, 10
challenges faced, 29
finding , 10–11
lowering stress level when, 10–11
basic needs of humans, 13, 28
less tangible, 28
Maslow's hierarchy, 28
beauty, being surrounded by, 138–139
in the community, 138
in the home, 138
as a philosophy of life, 139
preserving for future generations, 139
turning into a passion, 139
best, giving your, 161–162
challenge of, 162
taking time to improve, 162
what's required of, 162
Billings, Josh (humorist), on
persistence, 133
blackboard, using for writing, 7
blame, turning to when unpleasant events
occur, 76–77
blaming others for control over destiny, 3
body, and changes in from growing older,
49–50
bonding, with new relationships, 105–106
book group, joining a, 120
books, can help when facing crucial life
issues, 8
brain
learning new things aids in mental
sharpness, 51, 52
stimulating mind to stay active, 58
brainwashing by advertisers to sell
products, 77–78
budget. See also expenses
determining expenses, 27–28
living on fixed prior to retiring, 29
setting up a, 27
budgeting for retirement, 24–25
factoring costs of long-term medical
care, 25
factoring for inflation, 25
other factors to consider, 25
volatility of marketplace and, 25
burglars, protection against, 45

busy, keeping. See also time
with meaningful activities, 18

calcium, using oyster shell for stronger
bones, 54
Campbell, Joseph (author), on following
your passion, 129–130
cancer
exposure to radiation and, 60
green tea, drinking may reduce risk
of, 55
healthy diet to reduce risk of, 60
quitting smoking may reduce risk of, 54
cardiopulmonary resuscitation. See CPR
caregiver
being for parents and other older
people, 100, 101
finding assistance for, 101
cars
car rental agencies offering senior
citizen discounts, 33
carjacking, protection against, 45
driving, safety measures for, 61
theft of, protection against, 45
causes, becoming involved with
worthy, 131
Celestine Prophecy, The (Redfield), 39
certificates of deposit (CDs), and interest
rates, 34
change, continuing to, 157–158
not postponing making positive, 158
changes brought on by retirement, 4–5
aging process, physical and emotional,
6–7
identifying goals, 5
implementing, 5
needs of others, taking into account, 5
setting priorities, 5
status quo, not settling for, 5
children. See also family
giving money to, 39
not promising a large inheritance to,
24, 37–38
Choice in Dying (organization)
provider of do-it-yourself forms, 42, 66
Web site, 42, 66
cholesterol, high
lowering with high-protein diet, 54, 56
ways to lower, 54

choosing retirement as personal choice, 3–4
chores
    exercising when doing, 59, 114
    finding shortcuts to make life easier, 13
clutter
    cutting back on buying "stuff" that
        becomes, 141
    in home, 138
    junk mail, 141
    organizing, 140
    out of control, 140
    reducing, 139–141
Coenzyme Q10 (supplement), 55
commitments
    honoring to yourself, 17
    making meaningful with free time,
        16–17
    retirees offering suggestions for
        making, 17
complexities in life, ridding unnecessary, 13
compulsion to acquire things, why hard to
    change, 37
computer. See also Internet
    for e-mail, 121
    for health matters, using, 50
    for hobbies and interests, using, 122
    for legal affairs, using to take control
        of, 43
    learning to use a, 120–122
    for maintaining long-distance
        friendships, 91
    personal finance programs on, 28, 121
    for photo images, 122
    time demands of, 122
    for word processing, 121
    for writing life story, 122, 123
    for writing to people, 7
consumer, savvy, 31–33
    example of, 32
    junk mail, stopping, 32–33
    telemarketing scams, beware of, 32
    what it means to be a, 31
consumerism
    not going overboard on, 36–38
    recognizing brainwashing to buy
        products or services, 77–78
contemplation
    examples of, 119
    expanding mental abilities through,
        119–120

cooking, preparing own food, 56
counseling
    for depression, 6
    for facing crucial life issues, 8
    for help with fears, 81
    for help when stuck in grief process, 84
CPR (cardiopulmonary resuscitation),
    learning, 61
creativity, expressing through activities, 114
credit cards
    shopping online with, 32
    some offer free messaging service, 32
crime
    burglary, protection against, 45
    business investment schemes, 44–45
    car theft, protection against, 45
    carjacking, protection against, 45
    financial con artist, 44–45
    lowering risk of, 44–45
    pickpockets, protecting against, 45
    pursesnatching, protection against, 45
    violent, victims of, 45
cultural events
    attending, 124
    benefits of, 124
    having access to, 138
curiosity, heighten, 151–152
    ways to, 151–152

daily routines, will be different in
    retirement, 158
Darrow, Clarence (lawyer), on
    retirement, 99
death. See also dying
    accepting as part of life, 10, 81–82, 84
    how other cultures view, 82
    in denial about, 82
    making arrangements, 82
decisions, making
    evaluating options before, 14–15
    listening to both rational brain and
        intuitive heart when, 4
depression
    seeking help for, 6
    unhappiness may lead to, 148
destiny, having control over, 3–4
diabetes, avoiding sugars, 54
diet
    altering to meet special physical
        needs, 56

diet, *Cont.*
    healthy, 55–57
    paying attention to, 55–57
    playing vital role in quality of life, 15, 65
    preparing own food, 56
    vegetables, including plenty in, 54
Direct Marketing Association (DMA),
    32–33
    junk mail, contacting to stop, 33–33
    take name off calling lists, contacting
        to, 32
disappointments, not dwelling on, 134
Disraeli, Benjamin (British politician), on
    taking action, 131
Dome Home Budget Book (personal
    finance program), 28
donating money
    calculating how much to give, 39
    charitable gift account, 40
    as part of legacy, 40
    to worthwhile causes, 38–39
dreams, personal
    being honest and realistic in trying to
        achieve, 15
    finding new ones in retirement, 18
    finding time to pursue, 154
    finding worthy, 18–19
    helping mate achieve, 96–97
    pitfalls in realizing, 19
    retirement as time to work towards, 15
    staying focused on, 117
driving a car, safety measures, 61. *See also*
    cars
drugs, prescription. *See* medications
dying. *See also* death
    decisions to be made when, 67
    hospice care, 67

Earthwatch Expeditions, for volunteer
    opportunities, 118, 125
Elderhostel, 115, 118, 125
Einstein, Alfred (physicist), on curiosity, 152
e-mail, learning how to use, 121
emergency situations
    CPR, learning how to administer, 61
    heart attack, what to do when
        someone is having, 61–62
    knowing what to do in, 61–62
emotional health
    basic emotions, awareness of, 71

developing an open mind, 73–74
developing positive attitude about,
    73–74
learning to live happily, 72–73
modifying negative attitudes to
    improve, 71–72
regulating to enhance life span, 71–72
taking care of, 50
endeavors, new
    doing homework first, 117
    focusing on the dream, 117
    start with small changes in daily life, 117
    taking small steps when undertaking,
        116–117
energy, exercising will give, 60
engaged, staying, 155–156
    barriers to, 156
    broadening social contacts, 155–156
    how to, 155
enhancing activities, engaging in, 14
Enneagram (personality typing system), 10
environment, healthy, 60–61
    air and water quality, importance of,
        60–61
    chemicals and pesticides, 60
    living in a, 60–61
    radiation, 60
erectile dysfunction syndrome (EDS),
    treatments for, 94
Erikson, Eric (psychologist), on leaving a
    legacy, 39–40
estate planning
    charitable gift account, 40
    disbursement of tangible assets, 40
    executor, appointing, 41
    legal-financial expert, using, 43
    living trusts, 42–43
    wills, 42–43
executor for estate, having complete
    information on file, 41
exercise, 58–60
    aerobic, 54, 59
    benefits of, 58–59, 60
    doing as recreational activity, 114–115
    having alternative when primary
        unavailable, 59
    Kegel, 94
    routine chores, doing when
        undertaking, 59, 114
    for sagging face, 7

stretching, 59
studies done showing positive effects
of, 58–59
vital role it plays in quality of life, 15
walking, 53, 59
workout options, 59
expectations for retirement
being realistic, 19
having high, 147–148
not having low, 147–148
expenses. *See also* budget
reducing, 25
setting up a budget to determine,
27–28
tracking with personal finance
programs, 28
typically higher in retirement, 24
typically lower in retirement, 24
experiences, being open to new, 117
eyesight. *See also* vision
changes in, 6
corrective laser surgery, 6, 49
magnifying glasses, 6
reading glasses, 6

face, aging process and, 6–7
facelift, 7
facial exercises to help, 7
sagging, 6
facelift versus facial exercises, 7
family
asking for help in facing fears, 80
asking for help in simplifying life, 13
giving money to, 39
loss of, 9–10, 81
maintaining contact with during
retirement, 102
myth of happy, 102–103
normal, having different meanings in
various cultures, 102
not dwelling on the past when
conversing with, 153
problems arising over issue of control,
102–103
talking with when facing crucial life
issues, 8
traditions, carrying on, 100
fantasies, expect realized dreams to differ
from, 19
fast food, giving up, 56

fat intake, lowering, 54
fears
asking for help with, 81
common ones
of meaningless void, 18
of not having enough money in
retirement, 23–24, 81
facing, 80–81
files, putting papers in to reduce
clutter, 140
using a file cabinet, 140
financial future, planning for, 24–25. *See
also* money
being realistic when, 25
detailed inventory of assets, having, 42
factors to consider, 25
monetary needs, predicting, 29
reviewing past expenditures before, 27
setting up a budget, 27
understanding investment basics, 25
fire safety, 62
forgive
being first to, 103–104
coming to grips with issues from the
past, 103
401(k) (retirement savings plan), 34
free things for senior citizens, taking
advantage of, 33
Freud, Sigmund, on libido, 93
friendships
asking for help with facing life issues, 8
asking for help with simplifying life, 13
being a good conversationalist, 93
having with all age-groups, 92
improve existing, 91–92
long-distance, maintaining, 91
loss of, 9–10
making new, 92–93
past, connecting with, 91
using volunteering opportunities to
make new, 92
frugal
becoming, 28
difference between cheap and, 28

gardening, as beneficial activity, 108
giving money, 38–39
calculating how much to give, 39
charitable gift account, 40
as part of legacy, 40

glasses
    magnifying, 6
    reading, when most people need, 6
goals
    evaluating all options, 14
    identifying when making changes, 5
    taking charge when setting, 11
Golden Eagle Pass, for discounts in
    National Parks, 33
government programs
    free or low-cost housing, 27
    for medical care, 26
    supplemental income checks, 25
    taking advantage of, 25, 26–27
    for veterans, 27
grandparenting. *See also* parenting role
    carrying on family traditions, 100
    different styles of, 99
    from long-distance, 100
    role, in retirement, 9, 99–100
    supporting parenting styles of
        children, 99–100
gratitude, showing, 75–76
green tea, drinking for health benefits, 55
grief process
    feelings experienced during, 83–84
    giving ourselves permission to
        grieve, 83
    seeking help when stuck in, 84
    understanding magnitude of loss,
        82–84
growth, personal, continue in retirement,
    157–158
guilt, avoiding when trying to change
    habits, 53

habits
    applying healthy, 52
    celebrating new healthy, 53
    ideas to help change bad, 53
    retirement, using time to change bad,
        52–53
hair, corrective measures for, 49
happiness. *See also* unhappiness
    books on, 73
    choosing, 72–73
    learning, 73
happiness, tips for
    accepting the aging process, 6–7
    finding in pleasurable activities, 113

looking more positively at people, 149
    saying yes to opportunities, 148
    seeking out other happy people,
        88–89
    taking control of destiny, 3–4
Happiness is a Choice (Kaufman), 73
Happiness is a Serious Problem
    (Prager), 73
Harvard University School of Public
    Health
    research on positive effects of social
        activities, 124
hazardous products, avoiding, 60–61
health. *See also* medical care and
    treatment
    becoming educated on subjects
        related to, 50
    making top priority, 53
    taking care of both physical and
        emotional, 50
    thinking in context of long term, 15
health insurance, 26–27. *See also*
    Medicare
    self-insurance, 30
    taking control of, 66
hearing loss
    may have negative effect on mental
        ability, 51
    as part of aging process, 7
    using specially equipped telephones,
        6, 7
    writing skills, honing to stay
        connected with people, 7
heart attack
    aerobic exercise, benefits of, 54
    quitting smoking may reduce risk of, 54
    taking aspirin daily to prevent, 54
    and type A personalities, 79
    what to do in an emergency situation,
        61–62
helping others, 130–131
    examples of, 130
    with one-on-one assistance, 130
    with problems, 8
heredity, having some influence on
    personality traits, 74
high blood pressure
    eating salmon may lower, 56
    high-protein diet, may lower, 54, 56
    stroking pets may lower, 106

high protein diet, benefits of eating, 54, 56

Hippocratic oath, 65

hobbies, exploring, 114–115
  benefits of, 115
  creative choices, 114
  doing something wild, 115–116
  educational, 115
  examples of, 114
  picking up one from the past, 114
  using the computer for, 122

home. *See also* housing options;
  relocation
  bringing beauty into, 138–139
  possible options to look for, 137, 138
  what makes a good, 137–138

home equity loans, avoid making, 29

hormonal imbalance, may have negative
  effect on mental ability, 51

hospice care, 67

hotels, offering senior citizen discounts, 33

household emergencies, measures to take
  for prevention of, 62

housing options. *See also* home;
  relocation
  free or low-cost from government, 27
  full-time travel, 141
  moving to new home in same locale,
    142, 143
  relocating, 141, 142–143
  retirement center, 142
  retirement communities, 141–142
  staying put, 141

How to Double Your Vital Years
  (Walford), 54

Hubbard, Kim (writer), on persistence, 133

Impotence, male, treatments for, 94

income, having enough for day-to-day
  expenses, 24

inflation, factoring in when doing
  financial planning, 25

information, using Internet to find, 121

inner voice, listening to, 77

insomnia, using melatonin to help with, 55

insurance. *See also* life insurance
  health, 26–27, 30
  for long-term care, 29, 31
  Medigap, 26–27
  re-look at needs, 30–31
  self-insurance, how it works, 30–31
  term life, 30

insurance companies, using fear tactics to
  sell policies, 78

intelligence
  evolves with age, 50–52
  exercising mental capabilities once
    retired, 51

interest rates
  on certificates of deposit (CDs), 34, 35
  on investments, 35–36
  on money market account, 34
  on personal savings, 34

Internet. *See also* computer
  to find information, 121
  shopping online, 32
  using to fulfill curiosity, 152

investing
  balancing returns with risk factors,
    35–36
  capital gains, 35
  categories for, 35
  common stocks, 35–36
  interest paid, 35–36
  lending money, 35, 36
  risks involved with, 36

IRA (savings plan), 34
  and Roth IRA, 34

irrational beliefs
  can control life, 77
  challenging, 76–77

James, William (philosopher), on
  wisdom, 100

journal writing, as way to help with life
  issues, 8

judgmental, becoming less, 10

junk mail
  consider as clutter, how to get rid
    of, 140
  how to stop, 32–33

Kegel exercises, 94

Kennedy, John F. (president), famous
  quote on giving, 39

kindness, expressing, 87–88

Kuhn, Maggie (founder of Gray
  Panthers), 128

aser surgery, to correct failing eyesight,
  6, 49

lawyers, using to handle legal and
  financial matters, 44

learning
  continuing once retired, 118–119
  hands-on-activities to facilitate, 119
  how to go about, 118–119
  organizations which offer
    opportunities for
      Earthwatch Expeditions, 118, 125
      Elderhostel, 115, 118, 125
legacy
  leaving a, 39–41
  setting a good example for younger
    generation, 40
legal affairs
  becoming educated on, 43
  durable power of attorney, 65, 66
  living will, 42, 65
  medical power of attorney, 42, 65
  organizing your, 41–43
  records, organizing, 41–42
  taking control of, 43–44
  using a lawyer, 44
letting go, learning how, 112
libraries
  using to fulfill curiosity, 152
  using to research learning
    opportunities, 118
life experiences, making a record of,
  122–123
  audiocassette, 123
  family slide show, 122
  scrapbook, 122
  using a video camera, 122
life insurance. See also insurance
  redeeming, 30
  term, 30
life issues, crucial
  books offering help, 8
  death of family members and friends,
    9–10
  helping others will help you, 8
  journal writing to help with, 8
  retirement offering opportunity to
    access, 8
  talking to friends and family when
    facing, 8
  using therapy to help face, 8
life, quality of. See quality of life
life, staying engaged with, 155–156
life's problems, facing with positive
  attitude, 77

lifestyle changes, making when it comes
  to spending money, 28
listener
  becoming a better, 89–90, 93
  qualities of good, 90
  techniques to become a good, 90
live in the moment, 152–153
  how to, 153
  viewing life as a gift, 153
living longer, average American
  comparison of 1900 versus 2000, 53
living trusts
  for maintaining personal control over
    financial matters, 44
  and wills, 42–43
living will, 42, 65
  do-it-yourself forms, 42
loans, avoid making home-equity, 29
loneliness
  being alone doesn't necessarily
    mean, 159
  and relationship to poor health, 50, 80
long-lived, being proud of, 11
loss, understanding magnitude of, 83.
  See also grief process
love, expressing, 87–88

MacArthur Foundation, studies on
  positive attitude related to good
    health, 50
  positive effects of exercise, 58–59
  retirees and productive work
    hours, 128
  successful aging, 155
magnifying glasses, 6
marriage
  creative solutions for enriching, 96
  enriching, having an, 94–96
  first year of retirement a challenge,
    94–95
  heading off problems, 95–96
  helping partner achieve personal
    dreams, 96–97
  sexuality and, 93–94
Maslow, Abraham (psychologist),
  hierarchy of needs, 28
Maugham, Somerset (author)
  on death, 82
  on good habits, 53

medical care and treatment. *See also* health
chronic conditions, 63
courses of treatment, understanding, 63–64
factoring in costs of when doing financial planning, 25
government programs, 26–27
hoaxes, be aware of, 64–65
majority of expenses usually comes last 6 months of life, 66
Medigap (private insurance policies), 26–27
options for high quality, 62–64
second opinions, getting, 63
surgery, knowing all the options, 64
medical directives, preparing, 65–67. *See also* legal affairs
medical establishment, have turned dying into profitable business, 66
medical treatment. *See* medical care and treatment
Medicare, 26, 27. *See also* health insurance
Part A, 26
Part B, 26, 27, 31
Medigap (private insurance polices), 26–27, 31
medications
hospitalizations per year because of problems with, 65
Physicians' Desk Reference, using, 65
side-effects may have effect on mental processes, 51
medicine, practicing preventive, 53–54
Medigap (private insurance policies), 26–27, 31
melatonin (supplement), to help with insomnia, 55
memories, putting together good, 133–134
creating a memory project, 134
ways to document, 134
memory loss, short-term, 7
mental abilities
expanding by reading, 119–120
expanding by writing, 120
focusing more on then physical abilities, 10
mental deterioration
aging process and, 51
learning new things may stop, 51
some causes of, 51
stereotypes about, 150
mentoring younger generation, as way to make new friendships, 92
Microsoft Money (personal finance program), 28
minerals. *See also* vitamins
absence of crucial may have effect on mental ability, 51
oyster shell calcium for stronger bones, 54
taking in higher amounts, 54–55
money. *See also* investments
basic truths about, 24
fear of not having enough, 23–24, 81
figuring out where it goes, 27–28
quote by Henry David Thoreau on, 21
taking in 10% more then you spend, 16
understanding personal relationship with, 23–24
will not bring happiness, 36–38
money market accounts, and interest rates, 34, 35
motor homes, traveling by, 125
mourning. *See* grief process
moving to new home, visualize living there twenty years when considering, 16
multivitamins. *See* vitamins
municipal bonds (savings plan), 34
Myers-Briggs (personality typing system), 10

National Park Service, offering discount pass into parks, 33
nature connecting with, 107–108
activities for, 107–108
benefits of, 108
gardening as vehicle for, 108
going to different locales, 108
needs, long term
basic, 28
monetary, 29
thinking through, 28–30
negative emotions, caused by irrational beliefs, 76–78
nursing home, 101
nutrition, poor
may have negative effect on mental ability, 51

Index

older generation, setting a good example
for younger generation, 40
older, growing. *See also* aging process
challenges of, 7
physical changes, 6–7
120-Year Diet, The (Walford), 54
open mind, developing an, 73–74
optimistic outlook on life, having an, 149
options, evaluating, 14–15
barriers to, 15
goals when, 14
procrastination and, 15
osteoporosis
oyster shell calcium to keep bones
strong, 54
strength training to help prevent, 54

paper trail, keeping a, 43
parenting role. *See also* grandparenting
adjusting to new, 97–99
changes in retirement, 9, 11
developing adult-to-adult relationship
with children, 98
financial help for children, problems
with offering, 98
making relationship stronger with
adult children, 97–98
parents, aging, helping to take care of,
100–102
passion
defined, 129
following your passion, 129–130
examples of, 129
pursuit of beauty may become, 139
self-imposed roadblocks to
following, 129
past, accepting the, 158
pension plans, 34
using as a savings plan, 34
persistence
developing more, 132–133
stages of, 132–133
personal finance programs, 28
Dome Home Budget Book, 28
Microsoft Money, 28
Quicken, 28
personal financial records, using software
to organize, 28, 121
personal savings, 33–34
certificates of deposit (CDs), 34

interest paid on, 34
and pension plans, 34
rule of thumb for, 33
tax-deferred savings plan, 34
tax-free savings plans, 34
ten percent surplus rule, 33
personality typing systems, using for self-
discovery, 10
pets
benefits of having, 106
considering for company, 106–107
factors to consider, 106
obligations of ownership, 107
philosophy, developing well-thought out by
acceptance of roles, 9
focusing more on mental abilities
then physical skills, 10
looking ahead, 10
new attitude towards aging, 9–10
photographs
using a computer for images, 122
videotaping old, 123
physical skills
changes in as we grow older, 9–10
focusing more on mental abilities
then, 10
Physicians' Desk Reference, 65
plastic surgery, to slow aging process, 49
pleasures
benefits of undertaking pleasurable
activities, 112
finding out what brings enjoyment, 112
increasing amount of in your life,
112–113
list of simple, 111–112
positive attitude
developing a, 73–74
importance in sustaining good
health, 50
maintaining when growing older, 7, 49
positive habits
applying new, 52–53
celebrating, 53
ideas to help promote, 53
power of attorney
durable, 65, 66
for medical decisions, 42, 65
present, importance of living in the, 152
priorities, setting once retired, 5

procrastination
    when deciding to make use of time, 154
    when making decisions, 15
prostate, saw palmetto may benefit, 55
Protein Power (Eades), 54
Public Pensions, supplemental income
    plans foreign countries, 26

quality of life
    consumerism, not expecting
        happiness from, 11
    diet playing a major role in, 15
    difference between high standard of
        living and, 11–12
    exercise playing a major role in, 15
    main ingredients needed for, 155
    relocation may raise, 101
    seeking to raise, 12
    what constitutes, 12
Quicken (personal finance program), 28

Randolph, John (American legislator), on
    importance of the present, 152
reading
    benefits of, 8
    classics on the Internet, 120
    joining a book group, 120
    quality books, 138
  to sharpen mental acuity, 119–120
records, putting in order, 41–42
    updating on annual basis, 43
    what to include, 41–42
recreational activities
    examples of, 114
    exercising when doing, 114–115
    exploring, 114–115
red wine, moderate use may be healthy, 60
Redfield, James (New Age author), on
    giving to others, 39
relationships
    finding new ones in retirement,
        105–106
    finding through exploring hobbies
        and interests, 115
relatives. *See* family
relaxation techniques, practicing, 79–80
    benefits of, 79
    different types, 79
    who uses, 79

religion/spirituality
    attending services from different
        cultures, 116
relocation, 137, 141–142. *See also*
    housing
    being realistic about, 142–143
    choices to consider for, 142
    evaluating potential move, 143
    fitting in at new home, 143
remarriage in retirement, 105
    prenuptial agreements, 106
resiliency
    benefits of, 157
    practicing, 156–157
    ways to enhance, 156–157
restaurants, only eating out on special
    occasions, 56
retirees
    difference between happy and not-so-
        happy, xii
    number joining ranks of, xii
    setting personal financial goals, 34
retirement
    concern over having enough money
        in, 23–24, 81
    daily routines, having different, 158
    developing a well-thought out
        philosophy, 9–10
    finding new dreams and activities in, 18
    having endless unscheduled time,
        viewed as worst part of, 18
    letting go of old roles, 9
    not being ready for, 18
    organizing legal affairs, 41–43
    as personal choice, 3
    revisiting childhood dreams in, 11
    simplify your life, 13
    as time for personal discovery, 10
    viewing in a twenty year time span,
        15–16
    working towards personal dreams in, 15
retirement communities, 101
    assisted living, 101
    range of services provided by, 101
Retirement Sourcebook (Smith), xi, 151
retreat, going on to escape
    consumerism, 37
roles
    grandparenting, changes in
        retirement, 9

roles, *Cont.*
letting go of old, 9
parenting, changes in retirement, 9, 11
Roosevelt, Franklin Delano (president),
famous quote on fear, 80

safety considerations, 60–61
putting safety devices in home, 61
when driving a car, 60, 61
safety deposit box, having inventory of, 41
salmon, eating may help lower blood
pressure, 56
savings. *See* personal savings
saw palmetto (supplement), 55
scams
becoming aware of, 43
business investment schemes, 44–45
financial con artists, 44–45
medical cures, 64–65
telemarketing, 32, 44–45
tip-offs regarding, 44–45
Scheibel, Arnold, on brain research, 51
scrapbook
putting together a, 122
as way to document good
memories, 134
seatbelts, using for safety, 60
self-discovery
retirement a time for, 10
using personality tests to help with, 10
self-insurance, 30–31
senility. *See* mental deterioration
senior citizen discounts
airlines offering, 33
car rental agencies offering, 33
National Parks, 33
sexuality
benefits of fulfilling sex life, 93
desire for sex, 93
enjoying, 93–94
physical problems, seeking treatment
for, 93–94
stereotype about old age and, 150
trying new things, 94
simplify life, 13–14
asking friends and family to help, 13
basic needs of humans, 13
becoming frugal, 28
chores, finding shortcuts to, 13
enriching routine moments, 14

reducing living expenses, 25
steps to help, 13–14
stuff, not going out and acquiring, 24
single, being, 104–106
challenges of, 105
desire to bond again, 105–106
women, percentage living without a
spouse, 104
small business, starting own, 126
factors to consider when, 126
smell, sense of, using different aromas
and spices to enhance, 7
smoke alarms, testing, 62
smoking cigarettes
benefits from quitting, 54
quitting, 52, 53, 54, 60
social gatherings
attending, 123–124
benefits of, 124
examples of, 123
social life, being enhanced by joining an
interest group, 115
social security, 26
formula used to calculate, 26
how funded, 26
solitude
activities to enjoy, 159
finding time for, 158–159
standard of living, knowing difference
between quality of life and, 11–12
Staton, Bill (financial consultant), on
donating to worthwhile causes, 38
status quo, not settling for, 5
stereotypes about old-age, 149–151, 156
books on recognizing and fighting, 151
most old people are boring and
monotonous, 150
most old people are decrepit, 150
most old people are sexless, 150
most old people are unproductive,
150–151
most old people become senile, 150
most old people live close to
poverty, 151
old age starts at age 65, 149–150
stocks. *See also* investing
common, 35–36
when buying thinking in a twenty year
span, 16

strength training for seniors
   benefits of, 52
   to help prevent osteoporosis, 54
   to help with arthritis pain, 54
stress level, lowering, 10–11
stretching exercises, 59
stroke
   transient ischemic attack (TIA), 62
   warning signs of, 62
Successful Aging (Rowe), 151
sun, using protecting clothing and lotions
   to minimize effects of, 60
supplemental income, 26. *See also* Social
   Security
   formula used to calculate, 26
   how funded, 26
supplements
   Coenzyme Q10, 55
   melatonin, 55
   saw palmetto, 55
surgery, knowing all options before
   undergoing, 64

taste, sense of, using spices to
   compensate for losing, 7
tax-free savings plans, 34. *See also* savings
   plans
taxes, software programs to help with, 121
telemarketing scams. *See also* scams
   "Do Not Call lists", requesting to be
      put on, 32, 45
   protection from, 32
   targeted at older Americans, 44
telephones, special equipment for, 6, 7
television viewing, developing good
   habits, 138
Templeton, John (financial adviser), on
   spiritual wealth, 25
therapy. *See* counseling
Thoreau, Henry David (writer)
   on money, 21
   on simplicity, 13
thrift stores, shopping at, 14
time
   challenges of making best use of, 24,
      153–155
   finding to pursue dreams, 154
   making meaningful commitments
      with, 16–17
   not procrastinating, 154

time for ourselves, having, 158–159
timers, using giant, 6
transition to retirement, allowing time for,
   4–5
traveling
   full-time, 117, 125
   natural attractions, seeing, 138
   with focus and spirit, 124–125

unhappiness. *See also* happiness
   blaming others, sign of 148
   may lead to depression, 148
   saying no to opportunities, 148
   why we choose, 72
United States Public Health Service
   objectives on improving nation's
      health, 53–54

varicose veins, treatments for, 49
vegetables, having plenty in diet, 54
veterans, government programs for, 27
vision problems, may have negative
   impact on mental ability. *See also*
   eyesight
visualize life in twenty years, 15–16
   investments, 16
   keeping in mind when considering
      moving, 16
   personal dreams, 18
vitamins. *See also* minerals; supplements
   multivitamins, taking, 54–55
void, meaningless, not letting retirement
   become, 18–19
volunteering, 127–128
   benefits of, 127
   Earthwatch Expeditions, 118, 125
   finding right place for, 128
   making new friendships when, 92
   opportunities for, 128
   realistic expectations for, 19
   starting own organization, 128

Walford, Roy (author), on vitamins,
   54–55
walking
   as good health habit, 53, 59
   in nature, 107
watches, talking, using for when eyesight
   starts to fail, 6
wild, doing something, 115–116

wild, doing something, *Cont.*
    examples of, 116
    trying a nude beach, 116
wills, 42–43
    living, 42
    and living trusts, 42–43
    maintaining personal control with, 44
wise
    becoming, 160–161
    decisions, making, 160
women
    caregiver role for aging parents, 100
    living longer then men, 104
work
    considering after retirement, 18,
      125–127

demands on time, 3
factors to take into account before, 126
finding a job, 126
new career, downsides of, 19
productive by retirees, 128
using personal connections to find, 126
World Wide Web. *See* Internet
writing
    journal, 8
    to help our mental acuity, 120
    skills, honing to stay connected with
      people, 7
    using a computer for, 7, 121
X-rays, keeping to a minimum, 60